MW01224222

SHOCK!

SUCCEED IN BUSINESS

The essential guide for business and investment

Thailand

**Bea Toews &
Robert McGregor**

TIMES BOOKS INTERNATIONAL
Singapore • Kuala Lumpur

Photo credits:
All photographs by Bea Toews

© 1998 Times Editions Pte Ltd

Published by Times Books International
an imprint of Times Editions Pte Ltd
Times Centre
1 New Industrial Road
Singapore 536196
Fax: (65) 285 4871   Tel: (65) 284 8844
e-mail: te@corp.tpl.com.sg

Online Bookstore:
http://www.timesone.com.sg/te

Times Subang
Lot 46, Subang Hi-Tech Industrial Park
Batu Tiga
40000 Shah Alam
Selangor Darul Ehsan
Malaysia
Fax & Tel: (603) 736 3517
E-mail: cchong@tpg.com.my

Printed in Singapore

ISBN 981 204 879 0

Contents

This book is dedicated to Michael, Michelle and Myra.

Introduction

In Thailand, it is said that there are three ways of doing things—the right way, the wrong way and the "Thai way". The objective of this book is to explain the Thai way of doing business.

Thailand is in a state of rapid transition and the changes since mid-1997 have made it a particularly challenging place in which to do business. Whether you intend to do business in Thailand in the capacity of a foreign investor, an importer or exporter of goods, as someone establishing a business in the country with or without a Thai partner, or as someone intending to work in the country in a managerial position, you need some knowledge of the way the Thai business world works.

Succeed in Business: Thailand provides background knowledge to help you navigate the Thai business world. Knowing a little about the country, its government regulations, its economy, its international relations, the business climate and the business opportunities available will help you conduct your day-to-day business in Thailand. If you think that you need more information on any topic, look at Appendix B for sources of information.

In Thailand, more than most places, attempting to understand the intricacies of protocol is important. As a foreigner, you will not be expected to have mastered every detail of the Thai way of doing things. On the other hand, it is easy to jeopardise your business negotiations quite unconsciously by perpetrating some cultural insult. By observing protocol in the workplace, you will not only avoid making inadvertent enemies but you will make lasting friendships and attain your business objectives as well.

If you have already decided to invest in Thailand in some way, *Succeed in Business: Thailand* will help you to meet government and cultural expectations. If you are in the process of deciding whether or not you want to work in Thailand, the information in this book may help you make the right choice.

Map of Thailand

CHAPTER 1

Thailand Overview

Thailand is a geographically blessed country lying in the heart of Southeast Asia. It is a large and densely populated country. At the moment, Thailand's workforce is in transition from unskilled to skilled labour.

Location and Size

Thailand has a large land area of 514,000 square kilometres (roughly the size of France). It is 1,600 km long from north to south and 780 km wide from east to west at the widest point.

> **Thailand—The Elephant's Head**
> In learning to draw the map of Thailand, Thai children are taught that the country is shaped like an elephant's head, with the trunk of the elephant dropping south towards Singapore and its ears pointed towards Cambodia.

Bordered by Myanmar (Burma), Cambodia, Laos, Malaysia, the Gulf of Thailand and the Andaman Sea, Thailand is strategically located in the centre of the Indo-Chinese Peninsula. Its less immediate neighbours include China, Vietnam, Singapore and Indonesia. The large population bases of neighbouring countries provide enticing markets for people establishing businesses in Thailand.

Geography

Thailand is made up of 76 provinces, which are located in the central, southern, northern and north eastern regions. The country has two sea coasts, one on the Gulf of Thailand and the other on the western shores of the Andaman Sea in the Indian Ocean.

Central Region
Bangkok, the capital of Thailand, is located on the flat flood plain of its largest river, the Chao Phraya, in the fertile central plain area. One of Thailand's major export commodities, rice, comes mainly from this area. However, industrialisation has decreased the importance of rice to the export value of the economy. As a result, though rice accounted for nearly 40% of total export value in 1980, it now accounts for less than 15% of Thailand's total export value.

Transportation of goods, especially of teak logs, rice and cement from the other parts of the country to Bangkok Port was river-based until 20 years ago. Today, this produce is more likely to be transported by road or rail.

North Eastern Region
The north eastern Korat Plateau is becoming an increasingly important area for cash crops though it has a brutal climate, which alternates between floods and droughts. Projects sponsored by the royal family have been initiated in this region to increase the earning capacity of the rural community of the north-east.

Northern Region
Chiang Mai is the second largest city in Thailand and the major city of this region. Like much of Thailand, the north is becoming increasingly dependent on the tourist industry. Chiang Mai has become a popular destination for foreigners and Thais who seek to escape the heat and humidity of the lower regions.

The slopes of the mountains of the north are wooded with teak, an export commodity of Thailand.

Southern Region

The south is a hilly to mountainous area rich in marine and mineral resources. Splendid beaches on both sides of the peninsula are a year-round tourist attraction. Excellent harbours dot the coastline.

Climate

Thailand has a range of climates, from the tropical south to the more temperate climate of the hilly regions in the north. It has two major climate types—a tropical monsoonal climate in the south and a wet savannah climate in the north-east. Both areas are hot and humid, with rainy seasons from May to October.

Historically, Thai culture evolved around the rhythm of rains which governed agriculture, especially rice growing. The rains are still an important influence and Thais anxiously await the blessings of the rainy seasons.

Much of the central region, however, is low-lying and flat, thereby being susceptible to flooding. Bangkok, built on the delta of the Chao Phraya River, is notorious for floods in the rainy season. When selecting an office or factory site in the central region, check the surrounding area for high water marks and evidence of sand bags to make sure that your site will not be flooded.

A Word on Air-conditioning
Beware of air-conditioned taxis, buses, buildings, theatres and offices. The temperature contrast between the hot humid day and the cold interior may give you a chill.

Oddly enough, there seems to be a correlation between the temperature of a person's office and his significance in the company. Offices of really important people tend to be extremely cold all year round. Therefore, if you are attending an extended meeting with an executive or a government minister, it may be advisable to bring along a coat.

Flooding can be a deterrent to doing business in Thailand. This flood in Soi Mahattai in the suburb of Bangkok had reached such a level after only an hour of rain.

The south of the country also suffers from floods though there has not been much publicity about it as this part of the country is less industrialised.

The temperature range in Thailand is between 13 to 40 degrees Celsius and most of the country is humid all year round. Average low temperatures are around 20°C and average high temperatures are around 30°C.

The sunny cool period between November and February is moderately hot and beer gardens spring up all over Bangkok at this time to cater to the swarms of tourists. This is the peak tourist season and the most pleasant time of the year.

The summer weather from March to June is hot but broken by a rash of public holidays, one of which is Songkran, the traditional water-throwing festival to usher in the Thai new year. Many people leave Bangkok to avoid the heat at this time, heading north to join families still living upcountry—as regions outside Bangkok are referred to.

Rains, for most of the country, fall in the period, June to October. The beginning of Buddhist Lent coincides with the start of the rainy season and monks stay in their temple areas during the three-month Lent period.

In comparison to its neighbouring countries, the climate of Thailand is neither harsh nor destructive. There are no hurricanes, tornadoes, earthquakes or volcanoes on its meteorological records.

Environment

The environmental situation in Thailand is not particularly good, with pollution being the major problem. In Thailand today, industrial waste is constantly dumped into rivers, coral beds are dying from sewage and overuse, and forests are degraded by logging. In addition, there are no restrictions on the use of fertilisers in agricultural areas, so both the soil and water are polluted.

Air pollution in the capital city of Bangkok is at a critical stage, with dust and particle concentrations averaging seven times more than recommended levels. Most of this pollution comes from a large and rapidly growing fleet of motor vehicles and dust from the city's numerous construction sites.

Fortunately, the Thai government is attempting to control the problem. Measures taken include the testing of trucks and buses for emissions, and the requirement that building companies drape construction sites in netting to cut down on particle dust drifting to the street level. The effect of these laws will depend on their enforcement.

Thailand is aware of the damage caused to the environment by the government, industry and tourists, for example, international disapproval of pollution at Pattaya Beach has led to clean up measures there. Thailand is also instituting energy conservation and efficiency measures, including stricter standards for lighting, air conditioning and the use of insulating materials.

To remedy the problem of air pollution in Thailand, all buildings under construction must be draped in plastic to cut down on the amount of dust. However, the Thais neglect the fact that much of the smog in Bangkok is actually caused by traffic emissions.

People

About 75% of people living in Thailand are Thai and 14% are Chinese. However, intermarriage has blurred this distinction. As fair skin is a mark of beauty in Thailand, having Chinese ancestry is considered desirable. As such, you may be struck by the fact that many people you meet claim Chinese ancestry. The other 11% of the population is made up of immigrants and workers from India, Sri Lanka, Burma and other countries.

A permanent expatriate community lives in Bangkok, many of whom speak reasonable Thai. You will find representatives from most European countries meeting regularly at restaurants, bars, clubs and embassies, many of whom have Thai spouses. They are an invaluable source of information on doing business in Thailand, as many of them are involved in export, import or manufacture, while others act as consultants to Thai companies.

Population Distribution

Bangkok, with a population of between six and eight million, is Thailand's main population centre. The next largest city is Chiang Mai in the north, with a population of less than half a million. In spite of the recent emphasis on industrial products, Thailand is still very much a rural country, with the majority of Thais living in small villages.

The population of Thailand passed 60 million in 1996 and is slowly increasing. Under the influence of measures by the government, annual population growth has slowed from about 3.6% in 1960 to 1.3% today. However, even with the radical slowdown in birth rate, the population of Thailand has more than doubled since 1975.

Over half the population is under 30 years of age, and this young educated population sector is a major marketing target. However, there are few very young children in Thailand because of the successful birth control campaign and many families have only one child.

Mechai and Population Control

Thai economist, Mechai Viravaidya, was so concerned about Thailand's rapid population growth that he decided to take an active role in promoting the use of condoms as a birth control measure. Mechai started his campaign roaming Bangkok's red-light districts and handing out contraceptives to prostitutes and their clients. Later, he moved his campaign out to the villages.

For two decades, Mechai was the driving force behind a population-control programme—considered to be one of the most successful anywhere. Mechai's name became so strongly identified with prophylactics in Thailand that a condom is normally referred to as a "mechai". Now in his 50's, Mechai is proud to be known as "Mr. Condom".

Mechai has been the leading figure in dealing with the AIDS problem, which the government initially refused to acknowledge for fear of damaging the tourist industry.

Mechai and other health workers raised the AIDS issue in lectures, public speeches and interviews. His campaign increased public consciousness to such a level that AIDS was reported daily in the press and it still is today.

In 1991, six years after Thailand's first full-blown AIDS case came to light, the government appointed Mechai as the minister in charge of tourism, information and the country's AIDS prevention programme. In addition, the government now actively promotes the one-child family.

In 1996, in recognition of his achievements, Mechai was presented the Ramon Magsaysay Award, the country's highest civilian honour, for his services to the public good.

Source: 20 Great Asians Asiaweek Homepage

Average life expectancy rose from 63 years in 1960 to 67 years in 1990. Women outlive men by three years. Less than 5% of the population is over 65 years of age, which indicates that the greying population is not a significant market at this point.

A change in the Thai family culture has raised concerns over the fate of the ageing population in Thailand. The three generation household that was common in Thailand a generation ago is disappearing as young people adopt Western ways. As they acquire wealth and possessions, the young leave their parents' homes to establish homes of their own when they marry. The current economic climate may temporarily reverse the trend to leave home but it is unlikely that the move to the nuclear family will stop.

Language
The official language of Thailand is Thai but the language has many distinct regional dialects. The dialect of the central region is the 'official' Thai, which is the language taught in schools, used in Bangkok and heard on radio and TV news broadcasts.

Chinese is also widely spoken and English is taught in primary and secondary schools. If you are lost in Thailand, an English-speaking person will not be far from you. In fact, with the wider use of English in the country, it is possible to get by in business with English alone. However, an English-speaking Thai translator will be an invaluable aid to your business activities.

As a foreigner to Thailand, the question you would ask is, "Should I learn to speak Thai?" Generally, if you have the time, it is worthwhile learning some basic Thai phrases from a good teacher rather than trying to cope with a lengthy list of words from a Thai language handbook. While you may want to display your Thai language skills, it is probably better to avoid using poorly-pronounced Thai to somebody who already speaks good English.

If your pronunciation is bad, a Thai will be too polite to tell you. You will create a better impression if you say a few words in Thai perfectly and tell them that you would prefer to speak in English—after all, their English is probably better than your Thai. They will be pleased by your effort and will be left wondering how much more you actually know

Religion

About 95% of Thais are Buddhists. The rest of the population comprises about 3% Muslims, and 2% Christians and others. Westerners have been trying to convert Thais to Christianity for hundreds of years, with limited success.

While Thais are tolerant of all religions, they have proved resistant to conversion and regard people without a religion with suspicion. It is not a good idea to proclaim your atheism, as communism and atheism are seen to be connected. The fear of communism has not been extinguished in Thailand yet.

The Thai king is regarded as the nominal head of all religions in Thailand, including Christianity. He supports the restoration and building of mosques and Indian temples as well as *wats* (Buddhist temples).

The influence of Buddhism on your work-year and workforce will be described in some detail later in the book. The number of days your staff goes on leave may be influenced by their religion—though they may observe Christian holidays in addition to those of their own religions if their boss happens to be a Christian. If some of your staff are Chinese, they may even celebrate a few Chinese holidays. The large number of public holidays is some compensation for the fact that most Thais do not receive public holiday entitlements.

Education

Until 60 years ago, education in Thailand was largely the realm of the wealthy, the upper class and the urban population. The rural population was barely educated. After the revolution, however, universal education was gradually introduced.

The current education system consists of four levels: one or two years of preschool, six years of compulsory primary education and six years of secondary education, followed by higher education. Secondary education has both a technical and an academic qualification system.

The eighth economic plan (1997–2001) stresses the connection between education and the quality of life. The entire education system is currently under review and the government believes that many of the economic ills of the country can be cured by improving education. One of the pressing needs in the country today, if Thailand hopes to survive competition from industrialised countries, is skilled workers, particularly engineers and technicians.

Work Ethic

As the economy develops, there has been a corresponding increase in demand for the young educated middle-class Thai who speaks and reads English. Until recently, this group tended to regard the workplace as a social venue and their jobs as a source of entertainment rather than a career. As well-paid jobs become more difficult to obtain, even young employees are reconsidering their attitude to work, although there is no equivalent to the Protestant Work Ethic in Thailand.

The older generation prides itself on loyalty to a boss, provided that the boss is protective of them. While there is no life contract between worker and employee, a long and caring relationship between the two parties can exist, if both parties know the rules and abide by them.

Infrastructure

Energy

Power is supplied by the Electricity Generating Authority of Thailand (EGAT). Supply is 220 volts, 50 cycles AC and is reasonable though power cuts often occur due to thunderstorms, accidents and excessive demand. Though expensive by Western standards, concessions on electricity charges can be obtained.

Energy consumption in Thailand has grown at a rate of approximately 10–12% each year since 1986, and it is predicted that the demand for electricity will double in the next 15 years. This estimate is based on projected growth rates of the economy of between 7% and 9% per year and has been revised to between 3% and 6% for 1997–2001 to reflect decreasing demand due to recent economic upheavals. Plans to construct power plants in both western Thailand and on the eastern seaboard have been put on hold until the economy recovers.

Energy is obtained from oil and natural gas, biomass, coal and hydro electricity. Biomass (firewood, charcoal, bargesse and rice husk) is domestically produced and oil and gas are imported, though domestic sources are now being developed. About 85% of the coal used is produced in Thailand while hydro electricity is both locally produced and purchased from Laos and Myanmar. Offshore oil fields in the Gulf and in the northern province of Kamphaengphet have added to domestic reserves and are being developed further.

Water

Water is reticulated in major urban areas but is not safe to drink. Ice is manufactured under government licence and is clean, as is bottled water.

Thailand does not have an adequate water storage capacity. It suffers from cycles of floods and water shortages as the rainfall reflects climactic variation. In dry periods, especially in the north, water may have to be delivered by tanker trucks. This can be expensive so you should budget for tanks and on-site distribution systems when based in these areas. Various projects to build more dams have been proposed but constantly run into environmental objections and other obstacles.

Water disposal and purification is a major problem especially in the rural areas where rivers are increasingly polluted because there is little enforcement of waste disposal laws. The sewerage system in most parts of the country cannot handle toilet paper.

Therefore, you should use the toilet wastepaper baskets for the disposal of paper.

Improved water supply and disposal systems are urgently needed in Thailand. Industrial estates, which will be discussed later in the book, often offer good water and sewerage systems as prime attractions to their areas.

Transportation

Bangkok Transportation   Bangkok traffic jams are infamous and being stuck in traffic for hours is not uncommon. Bangkok grew too quickly, developing a road system based on the existing canal (*klong*) network. As a result, roads are narrow and tend to flood, buildings are close to the roads and there is little parking space.

Private cars, motorbikes, *samlors* (small, three-wheeled taxis), taxis, buses and trucks all compete for the same piece of roadway. At the same time, pedestrians overflow the footpaths which are dotted with food vendors, merchandise stalls and other stalls. Footpaths also play host to parked motorbikes and piles of masonry from the ever-crumbling public and private infrastructure.

Overhead expressways and underground and overhead rail systems have been planned and started. However, any construction must be made over or under existing roads which causes further traffic problems.

The projects have been undertaken by private companies, some of which have run into difficulties. For example, the Hong Kong-based firm, Hopewell, has recently fallen well behind its original contract completion date and has pulled out the bulk of its construction forces, pleading financial problems and payment disputes. In October, the government scrapped the joint road and train project. A lengthy legal battle is predicted between Hopewell Thailand and its partner in Hong Kong.

If these projects are finally completed and if the government succeeds in its aim of halting the population growth of Bangkok,

Such traffic jams are typical during peak periods in Bangkok.

the traffic situation in the capital might improve. At the moment, however, when considering establishing a business in Bangkok, consider the transportation problems very carefully.

Transportation in the rest of Thailand is reasonable, with a road, rail and river network operating all over the country. Thailand is also a regional and international hub of air travel.

Thai Roads   Roads in Thailand are not as good as the ones in Western countries though the primary highways are of freeway quality. The greatest proportion of roads are secondary roads which, though surfaced, are narrow and are not well-maintained.

In addition, vehicles are often not in good condition and trucks in various states of disrepair move cargo around the county. Road regulations are not strictly enforced and drivers are careless. Trucks tend to be overloaded and accidents are frequent.

At one time, constant inspection ensured that drivers were adhering to load limits. However, these inspections proved very costly and the alternative solution was to raise each truck's allowable payload, thereby avoiding the necessity for road checks. To the foreigner, this might seem an unusual approach but not in Thailand, where the aim of the exercise is not to solve the problem but to stop the problem from being a nuisance.

Road accidents are the fourth biggest cause of death in Thailand. In 1996, 19,000 people were killed in road accidents. Of these, 13,000 were killed in accidents attributed to speeding and 2,000 to improper overtaking.

You can drive in Thailand on an international licence. Remember to check any road map you buy for the date—maps are not updated each year. Alternatively, you could hire a driver, which many consider a better way to travel. This is because, as a foreign driver in a Thai accident, you can become involved in compensation issues that go well beyond any notion of fault. Moreover, Thai drivers tend to concern themselves more with questions of affordability to meet claims.

Buses ply the entire country and carry mail, parcels, food, people and sometimes, livestock. They are a cheap form of transportation, though not entirely safe.

Thai Rail Thailand has a reasonable rail network that reaches most areas of the country. However, the standard of the track and the rolling stock is poor. Overnight train travel for sleeper passengers is comfortable and cheap, provided you are in no particular hurry. This is because services are infrequent and slow.

Rail has the potential for development and proposals to overhaul and improve the rail system as better and cheaper alternative to roads are constantly considered, then disregarded.

Thai Airports Traffic through Bangkok International Airport (BIA) and the three connecting domestic airports at Chiang Mai, Phuket and Ban Hat Yai is increasing every year.

The facuous tuk-tuk (or the samlor) is a cheap and popular form of transport in Thailand.

At the moment, BIA—the largest airport in Southeast Asia—is always crowded but adequate. The airport is about 32 km from town and can be reached by a taxi or airport bus.

Taxis at the Airport

While taxis around town will generally turn their meters on, thus avoiding the tiresome need to negotiate the fare in advance, the cab drivers at the airport often refuse to use meters, preferring to quote a fare that is about 50% above the metered rate.

If you encounter a problem negotiating with the taxi driver after arriving at BIA, you may wish to try your luck at the "departures" level one floor above. Quotations for a ride downtown from the departures floor are about 20% cheaper. Alternatively, you can wait at the Tourist Authority of Thailand (TAT) taxi stand, which tries to ensure that each taxi you take is safe and uses a meter—be prepared to pay a surcharge of 50 baht though.

Growth of traffic through BIA has been steady and shows no signs of abating, so BIA will likely reach its maximum capacity in the next few years. The construction of a supplementary airport to BIA is already under way to the south of the existing site but plans to finish it are constantly debated.

International Air Traffic BIA			
	Number disembarked	Number in transit	Total number of passengers
1992	5,600,180	1,799,710	7,399,890
1993	6,346,516	2,015,949	8,362,465
1994	6,840,368	2,244,146	9,084,514
1995	7,533,896	2,199,224	9,733,120
1996	8,135,439	2,081,750	10,217,189

Thai Airlines Thai Airways International is both an international and internal carrier. The airline formed strategic alliances with Air Canada, Scandinavian Airlines System (SAS), Lufthansa and United Airlines in 1997 to enable it to offer connections to almost anywhere in the world. The formation of a second national carrier has been given government sanction but has not been implemented as yet.

Customs officials take their jobs seriously and like everywhere else in the world, they can exert their bureaucratic privileges on the traveller to make a routine check an unpleasant experience. Be agreeable, but never offer a customs official money for favours. While rampant corruption exists at the ministerial level, Thai authorities may come down hard on any rule-breaking or attempts to bribe customs officials. A number of foreigners attempting to smuggle small quantities of drugs have received 30-year sentences at the Bangkok Prison (nicknamed the "Bangkok Hilton") in widely publicised trials.

The Thai government has made efforts to increase the ease with which people enter Thailand as part of their plan to increase tourist business in the "Amazing Thailand" tourist campaign of 1998–1999.

Water Transportation   Goods are transported by river, from upcountry to coastal ports for overseas shipping.

There are two main rivers—the Chao Phraya and the Mekong—which move commodities and people across Thailand. Concrete, sand, salt, rice and logs are among the items which move down the Chao Phraya River to the major international trade port of Bangkok. Though trucks have made inroads on river traffic, loaded barges towed by tugs are still a common sight in Bangkok.

Bangkok has a series of canals (*klongs*) which are linked to the Chao Phraya and the sea. Some Thais remember a time when Bangkok was called the "Venice of the East" because the narrow canals were the main means of transportation and commerce (floating markets). Over the years, many of the *klongs* have been filled for development projects and roads. However, this has disrupted drainage and contributed to the periodic flooding Bangkok experiences during heavy rains The few floating markets remaining on the *klongs* are retained as tourist attractions.

Goods can be exported from or imported to Thailand from other ports a little further down the coast. Some distributors prefer to use Laem Chabang (1992) which has three terminals and Map Ta Phut Industrial Port (1992) which also has three terminals— one for general cargo and two for liquid bulk cargo. These ports service the spill-over from Bangkok Port as well as the rapidly developing industrial estates of the southeast seaboard.

On the south western coast, on the Gulf of Thailand, is Songkkla Port which has two multipurpose ports and one container vessel facility. Phuket Port is on the Andaman Sea and has two berths for large vessels. The southern ports are designed to promote the export products and industrial estates of the region.

Communications

Post office   Surface and air mail services are cheap but unreliable. It is estimated that only 50% of parcels sent by ordinary mail

Barge traffic on the Chao Phraya River.

actually reach their destination. Phone, fax, electronic mail and any other forms of communication are relatively better means of staying in contact with the head office or for sending urgent and important messages.

Thais are casual when handling mail at the office. For example, the mail will often be left with a gatekeeper, who may or may not deliver it to your office or if you are in a complex, to someone else's office. It is worth implementing a rigorous procedure for mail distribution to maximise your chances of receiving your mail.

Telephone The country's telecom services are run by the three state agencies—the Telephone Organisation of Thailand (TOT), Communications Authority of Thailand (CAT) and the Post and Telegraph Department.

Telecommunications is still a growing industry in Thailand and there are an estimated 3.2 lines per 1000 persons in Bangkok and about 25,000 public telephones. This is one of the reasons for the phenomenal proliferation of mobile phones which are not only status symbols but are necessities for people caught in traffic jams or living in estates to which phones are not yet connected.

Locating someone's phone number can be difficult in Thailand. Telephone lines are bought in blocks by entrepreneurs who resell them. If you cannot find a business name in a phone book it may be that the business line is owned by someone else who has not legally changed the name of the owner yet.

The most reliable source of phone numbers is the regional English Phone Book, published by the Shinawatra Group. The phone book is published both in book and CD format and both are delivered annually upon request. You would have to apply to the Telephone Organisation of Thailand to get the directory and must be a subscriber before you get the book.

Internet   Thais have taken to the Internet. Ten new servers entered the market between 1996 and 1997, and the overall number of users is estimated to be about 200,000. Internet use is expensive in Thailand as the charge includes connection fee, monthly rent and cost per minute. However, competition is fierce and corporate rates are available. Shop around for the best server and rates.

A list of Internet sites with useful information on Thailand is included in Appendix B.

Media

Thailand enjoys relative freedom of speech, given the fact that the government is dominated by the military. The English press does not hesitate to rail against the government and does so on a daily basis. The main restriction applies to negative reports about the Thai monarchy.

The news is known to be censored during times of political unrest such as the uprising of 1993. Opinion varies, even among Thais, as to how much censorship occurs daily on the radio and TV, and in the newspapers. The Information Division of the Interior Ministry, which monitored incorrect information and warned offenders of their errors, was disbanded when Prime Minister Chavalit resigned.

Radio

Thailand has 480 radio stations, most of which report to the Public Relations Department responsible for Radio Thailand—the country's official radio voice for government information and propaganda. All other radio stations in the country are commercial.

At 8 a.m. and 6 p.m., the royal anthem is played on all radio (and TV) stations. It used to be customary to stop whatever one was doing and stand at attention as a sign of respect for the king. Today, most people do not observe this tradition, though a few older Thais still do. Take your cue from your business companions and do as they do. Apart from the royal anthem, programming on radio is similar to that of other countries—music and talk shows, and lots of advertisements.

Thais consider noise an enhancement to most environments. For example, at Ko Samui, a coral beach resort, a loudspeaker system broadcasts music most of the day, adding little to the atmosphere of the beach. Similarly, department stores and malls are a cacophony of competing radio and TV programmes.

Television

Thailand started providing regular television services in 1955, the first country in Southeast Asia to do so. Channels 9 and 11 are run by the government, channels 5 and 7 are run by the military and channel 3 is run by private enterprise.

Asiaworks, Thailand's first private satellite transmission facility was created in 1997 by a group of foreign television journalists and Thai investors to enable correspondents to produce news footage from a single office and ease the flow of news in and out of the country.

Programming is similar to that of most countries. Comedies, variety shows, talent and talk shows, and soap operas from China and USA as well as cartoons from Japan are very popular. Educational programmes, especially nature programmes, have recently been introduced. Sports programmes are eagerly watched, especially English and Asian soccer matches.

Cable TV is readily available and there are about 10 privately-owned Thai, Indian and English channels. The two English newspapers provide television guides for cable channels, as do the Thai newspapers.

Not all Thai families own TV sets, so it is common to see people watching television in the malls and other public spaces, such as the area next to a food stall. Many restaurants also install television sets to draw customers.

Print Media

The printing press was brought into Thailand in 1835 by missionaries. It was primarily used by the royal court and foreigners until 1932 when the level of literacy was greatly expanded. Today, some 4,000 printing firms exist in Thailand, most of which are dedicated to printing packaging and brochures rather than books. The technology is world class and takes advantage of digital technology and printing management techniques.

A wide range of newspapers is available. *The Royal Gazette*, established by King Mongkut (Rama IV) is still the official medium for announcing royal and governmental legislation and proclamations. The *Thai Rath*, the *Daily News* and *Matichon* are the three biggest Thai papers while the biggest Chinese paper is the *Sin Sian Yit Pao*. *The Nation* and the *Bangkok Post* are the two major English papers.

Magazines are growing in popularity and are available in Thai and English. Imported magazines are expensive and purchased by young middle class clients.

Books are not held in as high an esteem as in European culture, though some fine charity books are published with excellent picture quality and layout. Popular English fiction, especially adventure and crime stories, is translated into the Thai language soon after the English publication.

Summary
The frantic pace of economic development of the 10 years preceding 1995 outstripped the development of the country's physical infrastructure, particularly in the area of transportation. Perhaps the current sedentary pace of growth will offer the country the opportunity to catch up and complete some of the projects it already has on hand, instead of continually starting new ones.

Thailand offers the investor many attractions—a substantial domestic market, proximity to a large market in Asia, a young workforce and a government that encourages private investment. The main problems are poor infrastructure, a polluted environment and a workforce that requires training. The bright side to this is that the government recognises the problems faced by the country and is making attempts to remedy them.

CHAPTER 2

The Thai Government

The Thai Government could be said to be one of the problems of Thailand. Though the government has maintained a consistently pro-business attitude, it has also been very reluctant to allow foreigners to own property or control companies. A brief overview of the political system is necessary to illustrate the complexity of dealing with the government.

The Monarchy

Thailand was ruled by a benevolent monarchy for the most part of its history. Details of the dynasties are given in chapter 3 on Thai economic history. On 24 June 1932, the 500-year-old monarchy was challenged and overthrown by the military. The king went into a self-imposed exile and abdicated shortly thereafter, nominating his son as the next monarch. His descendant is Thailand's present king.

Thailand is considered a constitutional monarchy with the king as the head of the state.

Constitutional Monarchy

Between 1923 and 1997, Thailand, under a constitutional monarchy, has had a total of 16 constitutions. The date of the second constitution, 10 December 1932, is still celebrated as Constitution Day. Changes in government usually lead to a new constitution, where charters passed has an average life-span of only 4.33 years. The 16th constitution was passed at the end of September 1997, with the charter to prevent the government from meddling with the rights of Thai citizens.

Under the constitution, there is the formation of a two-house National Assembly. It comprises an elected parliament and a

Senate, which is appointed by the king in consultation with the Council of Ministers or the cabinet.

The Role of the King Today

The king is recognised as head of state, head of the armed forces, upholder of the Buddhist religion and upholder of all religions. He is still regarded as sacred and above reproach in his personal life and actions.

King Bhumibol became the ninth Chakri King in 1946 on the death of his elder brother, Ananda Mahidol. He has earned the respect and admiration of his subjects through his concern for their well-being. He sponsors the Royal Projects which try to provide alternative economic activities for people upcountry, which include experimental rice farms to improve rice growing, dairy farms to improve agriculture, and artificial rain making for drought-stricken areas.

The king's power is much greater than specified by the constitution because of the great respect the people have for him. In 1987, after a nationwide poll, King Bhumibol became "King Bhumibol the Great"—the third Rama to be granted the title since the dynasty began in 1782.

In 1996, Thailand celebrated the 50th anniversary of His Majesty's accession to the throne, a year-long celebration which demonstrated the Thais' love and respect for their king. The king has "a father of the nation" image which has kept Thailand on course during national upheavals. In fact, his intervention has prevented widespread bloodshed on several occasions. While an endless series of politicians are alternately recycled and disgraced, the one stable political element in the country since World War II has been the king.

For the business person then, the main importance of the monarchy in Thailand is the stability that King Bhumibol brings to the country. In the civil unrest of May 1992, he defused national tension when he stepped in to urge General Suchinda and the pro-democracy leader, Chamlong Srimuang to compromise. The king's words were enough to prevent further violence and effectively protect Thai democracy.

Most recently, in the 1997 constitutional debate, the king urged that organic reforms be passed in parliament as quickly as possible to defuse the anxiety felt by the entire nation about the economy and the future of democracy in Thailand. He has also asked the Democratic government to keep their oath to perform their duties with honesty, wisdom and determination.

Political Structure

Thailand has a Westminster-style parliament. The House of Representatives originates legislation and the senate reviews it. Elections must be held every four years but may be called more frequently. The prime minister is an elected member of parliament, appointed by his fellow parliamentarians.

Thailand has not had a stable government this century. The balance of power between the monarch, the army and the elected government shifts constantly. Between 1973 and 1976, a series of five prime ministers held power. After that, there was a period of relative stability between 1976 and 1993. The four years following it have been unstable, with a string of seven prime ministers heading the government.

There has been no stable government composition this decade. In the daily newspapers, one is likely to read that a certain high-ranking government official has just resigned or has been fired. A short time later you may find the aforesaid back in power, at the expense of his previous persecutor. To the outsider, the machinations of Thai politics seem endless. The leadership is a passing parade of recycled, almost identical figures.

Perhaps the main implication for business of the unstable political situation today, is that the rules change seemingly at random and without notice, as the government struggles to find a way out of its political and economic problems. For example, with the arrival of the International Monetary Fund (IMF) to bail out the economy in 1997, VAT was increased from 7% to 10% without consultation with the business sector. As a result, businesses had to adjust or face stiff penalties. An increase in the price of oil requested by the IMF was imposed and rescinded in one week, decreasing foreign investment confidence.

The fact that most of the changes in the Thai Government do not affect foreigners or foreign investment is attributable to the moderation of Thai culture and the basically pro-business stance of the government.

Political Parties

Currently, ten political parties are represented in parliament and another 18 parties are registered. As there are no dominant parties in Thailand, governments are coalitions of shifting alliances of parties and people.

The major political parties in Thailand are the Democrats, currently led by Chuan Leekpai who became prime minister in November 1997; the New Aspiration Party; the Chart Thai Party which was last in power; the Mass Party; the National Development Party; the Palang Dharma Party; the Social Action Party; the Solidarity Party and the Thai Citizen Party.

Generally, political parties are not ideologically-oriented and are more likely to be centred on the personality and views of the key figure in the party. In fact, the policies of almost all of the parties currently in power are ideologically indistinguishable.

Most parliamentarians believe in a free enterprise system, in which many of them actively participate. The simultaneous pursuit of political and business careers leads to endless conflicts of interest and accusations of corruption. The 1997 Constitution includes clauses which attempt to prevent parliamentarians from becoming "unusually wealthy" as a result of government activity.

Elections

Elections are more individual than party orientated. Unlike other countries, the political parties in Thailand have no tangible identity. Candidates who are already in power and those who have influence or wealth have the best chances of winning seats. Many candidates do not even bother joining parties at all. Instead, they stand as independents who drift in and out of coalition partnerships as their personal circumstances and aspirations for power dictate.

Pollwatch recorded over 5,000 complaints of electoral violations, more than half of which involved vote buying, and reported an increase of 50 billion baht in circulation during the six weeks leading up to the November 1996 election. The September 1997 constitution, if implemented, should prevent a recurrence of such incidents.

Provincial Governments

There are 76 provinces in Thailand, each headed by a provincial governor. The office of provincial governor is the vital link between Bangkok and the upcountry populace, via the channel of the Ministry of Interior—to whom all governors report.

The National Assembly

The National Assembly comprises the House of Representatives and the Senate.

According to the constitution, the right to form a government belongs to the party winning the largest number of seats in parliament. The immediate problem confronting the core party is one of arithmetic, that of hammering together a coalition of parties to control more than half the number of the parliamentary seats. This can be a complex task as each coalition partner will require a price to join the majority alliance.

House of Representatives   Each of the 76 provinces must elect at least one person of at least 25 years of age to the House, which has a total of 360 members. The term of office is four years.

The Senate   The Senate consists of 270 Thai nationals over 35 years of age appointed by the king. These people neither belong to a political party nor act as consultants to any party, and are not in government themselves. Their term of office is four years.

Business and the National Assembly   Since the 1950s , the number of businessmen turned MP has increased and the preoccupation of the government has been with the economy. A plethora of economic development plans has continued to draw politicians into business and vice versa.

In the 1997 parliament, slightly more than half of the politicians (53%) were directly involved with business activities as owners of companies, partners, advertisers or brokers. The rest were mainly lawyers, former civil servants and farmers. Whatever their current occupations, many of the parliamentarians also had connections and past employment with the military.

The Cabinet

At the national level, executive power is administered and legislated by the cabinet in which all 13 ministries as well as the Office of the Prime Minister and the Office of State Universities are represented. A minister, together with one or more deputy ministers, will sit in the cabinet and form committees such as the Cabinet Economics Committee and the Cabinet Social Committee. For the coordination of major policies, the cabinet is chaired by the prime minister.

Important ministries like the ministries of Interior, Communications, Industry, Commerce and Agriculture are highly coveted for they control large budgets and award billions of bahts in government contracts.

The position of Minister of the Interior is cherished by ministerial aspirants because of the power that can be wielded over virtually the whole country through the local government apparatus. This large department controls agencies such as Local Administration, Land, Public Works and the Police as well as state enterprises such as Expressway and Rapid Transit, Provincial Electricity, Metropolitan Waterworks and National Housing.

As the Ministry of the Interior comprises 76 administrative districts, it is considered too demanding for one person. The responsibility is shared, sometimes among several different people. The Ministry of the Interior thereby serves as a convenient supply of ministerial positions for politicians who require ministerial status before granting support to the majority coalition. In 1997, there were five members from the Ministry of the Interior on the cabinet.

The allocation of cabinet seats inevitably causes friction and destabilises coalitions from the start. The first level of friction is between the parties who comprise the coalition—the November 1997 cabinet consisted of representatives from the Democrats, the Chart Thai Party and the Social Action Party.

The next level of friction is within political parties themselves. For instance, the Democratic Party tried to prevent Suthep Thueksuban from joining the cabinet on the grounds that he was responsible for the downfall of the Democrats in 1995 through the land reform scandal in which land which should have gone to poor farmers went to party members and associates instead.

The resulting cabinet is a consequence of arithmetical allocation within the coalition partners. The question of whether ministers are suited by talent or experience to their portfolios cannot be fitted into this equation.

Ministries that Influence Business Decisions

Office of the Prime Minister (ranks as a ministry)   It is largely concerned with the formulation of national policies.

It has a number of subdivisions:

- The Bureau of the Budget prepares the nation's annual budget.
- The National Economic and Social Development Board frames long-term development plans.
- The Juridical Council drafts the nation's laws.
- The Ministry of Justice administers laws after their promulgation.

Ministry of Industry The role of the Ministry of Industry includes the formulation of manufacturing and mining policy, the issuance of licences to factories and mineral leases, the formulation and supervision of industrial standards, the provision of technical assistance (especially to small scale industries) and the supervision of the Small Industries Finance Office.

Ministry of Commerce This ministry regulates external and internal trade, including the control of strategic commodities such as rice, the restraint of strategic imports and the provision of export promotion services.

Ministry of Interior This is the largest department and includes the Police, Immigration, Public Works, Town and Country Planning, the Local Administration Accelerated Rural Development, the Community Development and the Land Department.

Ministry of Agriculture and Cooperatives This ministry is responsible for the farming, fishery and forestry industries. The recently created Cooperative Promotion Department has also gained increasing importance in the last few years where increased agricultural productivity has been achieved by helping farmers to pool resources and realise economies of scale.

Ministry of Communications   It controls licensing and planning for land, sea and air transportation, as well as telecommunications services, including post and telegraph services, and the Internet.

Ministry of Education   The Ministry of Education oversees the administration in elementary and secondary schools, teacher training, and the restoration and cataloguing of fine arts. It is also in charge of Religious Affairs.

Government Stability

Curiously, commercial life goes on mostly uninterrupted against this restless background of political intrigue and corruption. Despite the changes in the government over the years, Thai economic policies have remained remarkably consistent—characterised by an openness to the outside world, sympathy to the strategic objectives of the United States and the West, fiscal conservatism, and a preference to let the private sector do what it does best.

There is no significant segment of the Thai political spectrum that disagrees with these policy fundamentals. For these reasons, Thailand's economy—together with the confidence of the domestic and foreign private sectors—has shown consistent growth, at least until the downturn of the mid-1990s. If handled in accordance with IMF ruling, the setback could be short-lived and the economy could become one that is more productivity-based and stable.

Problems in the Government

The main problems of the Thai Government are the frequent and corrupt electoral process, the levels of corruption in the government itself, and the intricacy of the bureaucracy. Though the first will not affect your business, the others will.

Deficiencies in the Thai Political System
The *Bangkok Post* summary of the deficiencies it sees in the Thai political system are as follows:

- Senators are appointed as rewards for service.
- All members of the House of Representatives all come from the same background and it is, therefore, not representative of the nation.
- Elections are rigged.
- Coalitions are not effective governments.
- Business people-cum-politicians are subject to conflicts of interest.

Source: *Bangkok Post*, 20 October 1996

The Electoral Process

Elections are held frequently in Thailand and can be very costly affairs. The high frequency of elections leads to confusion and uncertainty, and as more and more sectors of the community start to demand government responsibility and accountability. Frequent elections seem likely to continue.

The Process
"Candidates for the new parliament win their seats through widespread vote buying. Upon entering the parliament, they must therefore concentrate first on repaying their financiers and supporters. Then they must find ways to obtain money for the next election. Only then can they focus on the problems of the country, but when they do, they only concern themselves with immediate problems, not the more important long term problems that must be solved if the country is to progress. Finally, after a short period, parliament is dissolved and the cycle repeats."

Source: *Bangkok Post*, following 1996 election

Farmer unrest, student protests and labour strikes are constant features of Thai civil life. The inability of each successive government to provide a lasting constitution and remove military interference have become constant features of Thai political life. Since 1973, two coups have been staged but were unsuccessful in bringing any lasting improvement to the political system.

The Coalition

In May 1992, pro-democracy political parties and non-governmental organisations initiated peaceful demonstrations that turned violent when the military interfered. After six months of political uncertainty, free and fair elections took place in September 1992 where a coalition was formed by Prime Minister Chuan Leekpai.

This coalition was soon reshuffled in September 1993 when a new partner replaced one of the original five parties that formed the coalition. For a while, the coalition succeeded in restoring domestic and foreign economic confidence in Thailand through its pro-democracy and pro-market stance.

PM Chuan was replaced shortly after by a new series of leaders in the more traditional mould. However, true to the unpredictability and uncertainty in the Thai electoral process, PM Chuan is now serving a second term of office in 1997, following the currency crisis in the same year.

Corruption

A 1995 *New York Times* survey, based on the perception of business executives and journalists, attempted to quantify the comparison of corruption in various countries according to a "Corruption Index". Six out of the most corrupt countries surveyed were in Asia and the other two were in South America (no African countries were listed in the survey).

Thailand was the eighth most corrupt country in this survey, obtaining one of the lower Asian rankings.

Corruption Index

Country	Ranking	Corruption Index
Indonesia	1	1.94
China	2	2.16
Pakistan	3	2.25
Venezuela	4	2.66
Brazil	5	2.70
Philippines	6	2.77
India	7	2.78
Thailand	8	2.79
Italy	9	2.99
Mexico	10	3.18
Columbia	11	3.44
Greece	12	4.04
Turkey	13	4.10
Hungary	14	4.12
South Korea	15	4.29

Notes:
1. New York Times Survey, 1995
2. For the ranking of countries, most corrupt=1, least corrupt=44.
3. The higher the "corruption index", the lower the corruption.

A more narrowly-based survey was also made of 280 company executives working in 12 Asian countries. The objective of the survey was to determine if the level of corruption was increasing. In the opinion of those surveyed, corruption had increased for all the countries surveyed except Singapore and the Philippines.

Another view on corruption is that its level has not changed. In the opinion of some long term residents of Asia, corrupt practices that are now being exposed in the media are not really new. What is new is that they are only now being exposed. Practices quietly accepted in the past are now a source of much more public criticism, giving rise to the perception that corruption is increasing.

The growing tendency to expose problems that have long existed may be a reflection of change in Asia. Viewed optimistically, this could be an indication that Asia is maturing and that societies are less willing to tolerate practices that, just a few years ago, were accepted as part of the cultural fabric.

Viewed negatively, it could indicate that Asian economies have advanced to a level where the corruption will impede future economic development, and produce the social and political instability characterising Thailand of the present day. In most people's minds, today's economic problems are closely linked to corruption. The numerous scandals that surfaced in Thailand in 1996 that precipitated the collapse of the Banharn government have not abated. The ethical standards of the government that replaced the Banharn regime have not improved significantly and the Chuan government includes members who were previously associated with scandals.

However, the government does make the occasional desultory attempt to do something about corruption.

The Popsicle Project

On 1 May 1997, four agencies announced measures to ensure that government funds reach their intended projects rather than be "siphoned off by corrupt officials".

These measures became collectively known as the "popsicle project", where corruption was compared to a stick of popsicle licked by one official after another so that all that remained to be handed from the last official to the people was the "popsicle stick".

The plan calls for specific budgeting measures to ensure that the money goes to a specific agency and to a particular project. The plan will be implemented in the 1998 fiscal year.

The main effect that corruption has on business is in making licensing and customs unpredictable in extent and cost, and in making paperwork difficult and costly. Make sure that your adviser knows the correct way to obtain licences and other documentation.

Bureaucracy

The civil head of a ministry is the permanent secretary who has administrative control over the departments under the ministry, each of which is headed by a director-general, who is a career civil servant. Large departments are often split into divisions which may be subdivided into sections. As in many Western countries, employment in the public service is a job for life, with both security and prestige. It is extremely difficult and unusual for a non-Thai to be included in the Thai Government workforce.

Thailand has been assessed by international executives as being among Asia's five most inefficient bureaucratic systems, along with Vietnam, Indonesia, Myanmar and Cambodia. The Thai Rating and Information Service, set up to monitor the efficiency of the civil service, may help to alleviate the problem of information being processed too slowly. However, as the body was only set up in 1997, it is far too early to predict its effectiveness.

Interacting with the Bureaucracy   As a foreigner in Thailand, you will be required to sign many documents in the Thai language. One of the first things to do is to find a person proficient in the Thai language to translate these documents for you. If you can, take your translator with you on visits to government offices.

Take note that the Thai bureaucracy requires your passport photograph affixed to most of the forms they give you, so have a large supply of passport-sized photographs on hand. That Thailand spends such a small proportion of GNP on government services does not indicate a shortage of officials. Rather it indicates that the government bureaucrats you will doubtless encounter are poorly paid.

Legal System

The constitution guarantees fundamental rights to every Thai citizen. Other laws are formed at various levels of the administrative hierarchy—the monarch, the parliament and the various ministries—and carry titles that depend on the issuing authority, for example, a code, an act, an emergency royal decree and a ministerial regulation.

The Ministry of Justice was established in 1892 to protect the rights and entitlements of citizens against actions by the state. Civil disputes, such as the enforcement of property or contract rights, are resolved through Thai courts in a manner similar to other countries.

By and large, Thailand does not recognise foreign judicial judgements unless they are covered in some previous agreement with the issuing nation. At present, Thailand is not a member of the International Centre for the Settlement of Investment Disputes. Therefore, foreigners may not enforce a judgement made in their country. Instead, they must begin a new law suit in Thailand, which can prove to be a slow and costly process.

The Arbitration Act was passed in 1987; arbitration has become an increasingly popular form of settlement due to its convenience, informality and quick judgements. For international disputes, this act may recognise the arbitration finding of a foreign court under certain circumstances.

Jurisdiction of the Courts

The Thai Courts of Justice are divided into various categories:

- The civil court called the "court of first instance"
- The criminal court
- The juvenile and family court
- The central labour court
- The central tax court

- The *kwaeng* courts, which have jurisdiction over minor civil cases and criminal cases (the maximum punishment is imprisonment not exceeding three years or a fine not exceeding 60,000 baht, or both)
- The provincial juvenile and family courts in the provinces
- The various courts of appeal (three regional courts and one Bangkok Court of Appeal)
- The supreme court, which has the right to review and adjudicate all cases

The decisions reached by appeal courts are final, except in criminal cases where the accused may appeal to the king.

In addition to civil jurisdiction, there are also Military Courts which you, as a foreigner, should never need to face.

The legal principle that the accused is innocent until proven guilty applies in Thailand—at least in theory. The accused has the right to defend himself or herself, including the right to have a counsel.

However, the entire legal system is hopelessly clogged with unresolved cases. As a result, many cases are not heard, particularly if charges are minor. For example the number of amphetamine dealers who get to court is small compared with the number who are arrested, as is the number of people who have been convicted of VAT fraud.

The Police

The Police Department is not a part of the Department of Justice. This section has been included because of the apparent connection between the two arms of the law. Traffic police on motorcycles wearing surgical masks are stationed at most major intersections to "untangle" Bangkok traffic and curb over-enthusiastic traffic behaviour. It is difficult to associate the ubiquitous policeman with reports of police violence that feature in local news.

Accounts of people being killed before reaching the police station are not uncommon. An example is the incident of 27 November 1997, where six suspected amphetamine dealers were killed by police. The families of the victims are currently in the process of suing the government and are demanding compensation for the loss of their breadwinners.

Corruption in the Police Force
"There's nothing under the sun that Thai policemen cannot do. The police station here [at Lang Suan] functions like a big company. There are over a hundred staff. Ten percent of them are clean. The rest are involved in some kind of network."

Source: *Bangkok Post*, 6 July 1997

Under present legislation, suspects who are arrested can be detained indefinitely without prosecution or hearing. A 1997 constitutional amendment proposed that police should have the right to detain suspects for a total of only 24 hours. However, this proposed amendment is opposed by the police who fear an erosion of their power.

The police also possess the power to detain and question anyone. Foreigners can actually be fined for not having their passports with them in a public place. One middle-aged foreigner known to the authors was walking down the street when he was stopped by police who asked for his identification and body-searched him because "his face looked excited".

The harassment of aliens suspected of possessing incorrect business licences is also common. This is particularly the case for industries where the government wants to discourage foreign participation without actually banning it.

On Operating a Go-go Bar

First and foremost, the government demands of the Go-go bar, not one, not two, but 28 licences! The paperwork involved (all applications are in triplicate) is mountainous.

Even when correctly filled out and properly submitted with the requisite fees, getting the paperwork signed, stamped and approved adds a new dimension to the term "red tape". Some lucky people have their licences granted in weeks while others only get theirs after a few months—some do not get replies at all. Meanwhile, the establishment with a rent paid up opens and operates without proper documentation.

At this point, the constabulary arrives, notes the absence of the required licences and threatens to close the ale house for running illegally. However, *baksheesh*—the local slang for bribe money—prevents the police from carrying out his threat and the saloon-keeper is told to re-submit his applications. This is done, with the same lack of results and the police return—which explains why the vast majority of "oases" in Pattaya and many in Bangkok do not have operating licences.

Until you get someone with influence to assist you, you may never get all the licences required. As a rule, licences do not have an expiry date. Still, if you do manage to acquire them, there is nothing to prevent inspectors from coming around and declaring that certain licences have to be renewed annually and others, every six months.

Source: *Bangkok Post*, Nite Owl, 14 June 1997

Foreign Policy

For over five hundred years Thailand has officially welcomed trade. In the current age of globalization, transparent borders and regional trading blocks, imports and exports play ever more important roles in the economy. Imports and exports increase each year as a proportion of GDP. Trade associations are also becoming increasingly important. The government encourages trading relations both locally and internationally.

Regional Trading Blocks

Thailand is a member of a number of regional and global associations of trading nations. They include:

- Agreement on the Common Effective Preferential Tariff (CEPT)
- Asia-Pacific Economic Cooperation Forum (APEC)
- Association of Southeast Asian Nations (ASEAN)
- Indian Ocean Rim (IOR) (Thailand is attempting to join this group)
- Mekong River Development
- South Asian Association for Regional Cooperation (SAARC)
- South Asian Preferential Trading Arrangement (SAPTA)
- South Pacific Regional Trade & Economic Cooperation Agreement (SPARECA)

Of these, the most important is ASEAN. It is with this group that Thailand does more trade than with any other in the region. The agreements affiliated with ASEAN are listed below.

ASEAN   The Association of Southeast Asian Nations (ASEAN) was formed by Thailand in 1967 and includes Malaysia, Indonesia, the Philippines and Singapore. Brunei joined the organisation in 1984 while Vietnam was made a member in 1997. Meanwhile, the groundwork has been laid for the admission of Laos, Cambodia and Myanmar (Burma) into the group—as soon as their political situations stabilise.

The objective of ASEAN is to promote an ASEAN Free Trade Area (AFTA) so as to lower tariff barriers between member countries. AFTA is to be phased in over the next 15 years and aims to increase trade among ASEAN members through the liberalisation of insurance, capital markets, finance, banking, telecommunications and tourism.

A specific programme aims to increase the market size, cut the cost of manufactured goods and speed up delivery of goods and services within the ASEAN area. Currently, the main impediments to trade between ASEAN member countries are taxes and inspections at borders, regulations requiring that goods be moved to different carriers when crossing borders and in the instance of Laos, different road rules and working hours. Recent initiatives include the reduction of import tariffs among member countries and the pooling of industrial development efforts through cooperation and mutual consultation.

ASEAN formed links with the United States in 1977 and with the European Economic Community (EEC) in 1980. The heads of ASEAN meet with trading partners annually. To date, the group has established links with agencies in Japan, Australia, Canada, New Zealand and the United Nations.

The Asia Pacific Economic Forum (APEC) is a broader-based trading group comprising all the ASEAN members plus other countries around the Pacific, including Japan, the United States, Mexico, Australia and New Zealand. APEC's 18 member countries hope to achieve free and open trade and investment throughout the region by the year 2020.

Foreign Policy on Individuals

The foreign individual in Thailand is bound by a series of immigration and business laws which make it frustrating and time-consuming to arrange a lengthy stay in the country.

The immigration laws of Thailand allow you to choose from a variety of terms of stay. If you are working in Thailand, your family can join you in the country. The main difficulties in obtaining a visa are the time it takes to process a work visa (about a year) and the expense of renewing short-term visas.

SUCCEED IN BUSINESS: THAILAND

Kinds of Work

Under current Thai regulations, only persons of Thai nationality may be licensed in professional services like accounting, architecture, engineering, construction management, brokerage services and legal services. However, foreigners schooled in these professions can obtain licences if Thai nationals of the appropriate levels of expertise are not available.

Thais admire foreigners for their efficiency and organisation. In some businesses, the English-speaking, multi-skilled foreigner is treated like a guru—until the novelty wears off.

Visas and Work Permits

Nationals from 56 specified countries can now stay in Thailand for up to 30 days without an entry visa. For visitors from 76 other countries, visas valid for 15 days may be obtained on arrival at any of the four airports (Don Muang, Chiang Mai, Ban Hat Yai and Phuket). There are many categories of visas, including transit visas, visitor transit visas, tourist visas, non-immigrant visas, immigrant visas and nonquota immigrant visas.

At the moment, the government is revising the structure and costs of visas to bring in more foreign currency. Phone the Thai embassy in your country to determine the kind of visa you require and the length of time you are allowed to stay in the country. Holders of transit, visitor transit and tourist visas are not allowed to work in Thailand.

Visa Validity	
Type of Visa	**Validity**
Transit Visa	One month
Tourist Visa	Two months
Non-Immigrant Visa	Three months
Immigrant Visa	One year

Other than employment, foreigners can enter Thailand to receive or give support to a Thai spouse or other persons who live in the kingdom, to receive support from Thai parents or relatives, to study Buddhism, to study in a government university or college, private college or private school or international private school, or because of illness.

Normally, a three-month working visa will be issued by the Thai embassy in the country of origin on behalf of any employees hired for the enterprise in Thailand. A letter from the hiring company inside Thailand giving reasons justifying the employment of the foreigner is required to support the visa application.

Once inside Thailand, this visa will have to be extended regularly. Extending the visa may be a long, arduous and repetitive process where extension periods granted seem arbitrary and short—usually one or two months, or sometimes only two or three weeks. Furthermore, up to 21 different documents may be required to support the application, together with the customary suite of photographs and a fee for each application.

On the other hand, work permits may, in some circumstances, be granted for a year and be subject to annual extensions thereafter. It is worthwhile for companies to persist in the requests for the annual work permits for staff rather than continually extending the three-month visa.

Visa Tips

A foreigner working in Thailand may spend a great deal of time trying to obtain a work permit and maintaining visa status. In some cases, the foreign worker may need to leave Thailand every three months if the work permit cannot be obtained.

Be prepared to have your foreign workers disrupt their work routine and leave periodically to renew their visas. Alternatively, you could provide visa services for them. This constitutes a real benefit for you and the worker.

Doing Business in Thailand, written and updated annually by Bangkok Legal Consultants, has detailed and invaluable information on visas and work permits.

Re-entry Visas

Those entering and leaving the kingdom must apply for re-entry visas each time they leave the country at a cost of 500 baht per re-entry. If your visa expires before you leave the country, you will be fined 100 baht per day for each day that your visa has expired. You can get a temporary 10-day extension from the Immigration Department for 500 baht. Multiple re-entry visas are also available. These cost 1000 baht a year—for as many re-entry visas as you need in that year.

Check the papers to take advantage of visa travel packages. The entire process can be completed in less than 48 hours if you have the right connections.

Permanent Residence

It is extremely unusual for a person to gain permanent residence in Thailand. The applicant must have a non-immigrant visa and must have lived in Thailand for two to three years. Supporting documents to be submitted with the application for permanent residency are the same as those for a non-immigrant visa. However, these documents must show that you can benefit the economy of Thailand, that you can bring extra funds from abroad, that no Thais can do the job in which you are employed, or that you are immigrating for religious reasons—in which case you will need a letter from your embassy (between 1 January–30 June).

Citizenship

In Thailand, the official policy on citizenship states that it is a birthright and can only be applied for by a person born in Thailand, whose father is a Thai national. Citizenship will not be granted if only the mother is Thai—the child will take on the nationality of the father. It is likely that this policy will change in the near future.

There are, however, some exceptions to this general rule. Foreign women who marry Thai men can obtain citizenship after five years and Thai women in the government structure can sometimes obtain citizenship for her foreign husband. The longer you live in Thailand, the more you will notice that there are exceptions to every rule. If you really want to become a Thai citizen, ask among your friends for examples of people who have done so and you might find a way to accomplish this feat.

Public Service

The Thai Government owns and operates about 65 state enterprises, mainly utilities, communication, transportation and other infrastructure companies. State-owned corporate enterprises employed 250,000 people in 1996, not including the one million civil servants directly employed by the government bureaucracy. Public sector employment accounts for over 25% of all salaried employment and 6% of the workforce as a whole.

The cultural attitude to working in the public service has changed over the years. In the past, holding a government position was considered a privilege. Now, educated civil servants are leaving the government and heading for jobs in the private sector as these jobs are perceived to be better.

The government ranks are also likely to be thinned by increased computerisation. Until recently, the typical tools of trade of a lower grade civil service were a wooden desk, a pencil and a vast range of ink pads. In sharp contrast, government offices today are heavily reliant on computers.

However, the current economic downturn has put pressure on government expenditure and on implementing efficiency measures and cutting jobs.

Summary

Thailand and its government is at a turning point today, imposed by the consequences of the 1997 economic downturn. For years, Thailand has successfully resisted foreign domination and adhered to the Thai way of doing business.

Now, although there is no indication that the overall policy will change in the immediate future, the International Monetary Fund (IMF) has become entrenched in the country, calling the shots on the economy. Clearly, the Thai Government is not comfortable with the prospect of losing some of its economic sovereignty. However, in the tradition of leaders past, it is cooperating publicly while pulling strings behind the scenes to maintain its own control over the country's treasury. For instance, the IMF called for the budget to be cut by 100 billion baht for 1998 but the prime minister cut the budget by only 58 billion baht—maintaining that it was enough and that the budget could be balanced by additional value added tax (VAT) collection.

Though there is a great deal of disquiet in the country with regards to the performance of the government and corruption at the political level, it is likely that business will continue relatively uninterrupted—if the recent past is any indication of the future.

CHAPTER 3

The Thai Economy

In Thailand, as in many Newly Industrialised Countries (NICs), rapid evolution of the economy still takes place. It is this swiftness of change that provides varied business opportunities to local and overseas investors. However, rapid change also presents risks to the business investor in Thailand.

In the past 30 years, the structure of the Thai economy has shifted from an economy based on agriculture to one based on industrial products like textiles, footwear, garments, toys and jewellery, and more sophisticated products like electronic components, petrochemicals, paper products, transport, iron and steel, and scientific products.

The present diversification of the Thai economy offers investors a varied investment environment. Investors can choose to invest in sectors like agriculture, manufacturing, or the steadily growing tourist and service industry.

Thailand has an open market economy based on free enterprise, where the private sector has been allowed to develop with relatively little supervision, other than bureaucratic procedures. At the same time, monetary and fiscal policies were conservative until the boom period. The interests of the Crown, the military and the bureaucracy are combined in a complex hierarchy, which at present promotes business in general and foreign investments in particular.

When *Thailand's Boom* was written in 1996, very few people doubted that the boom would be sustained. A year and a half later, the Thai economy was in jeopardy. A sinking currency, a fluctuating stock exchange, an oversupply of property and an uncertainty in the entire financial system were identified as the chief reasons for the collapse of the economy. Like other countries that have restructured and recovered from apparently irrecoverable situations, Thailand, too, can recover by learning from the experiences of these other countries. In this way, it can develop its strengths, correct its weaknesses and eventually pull through the crisis.

Economic History

Agriculture in Siam began about 10,000–20,000 years ago. By about 10,000 BC, cattle, pigs and chickens were domesticated and rice was cultivated. Metallurgy in copper and bronze dates as far back as 5,000 years while iron and pottery date back 3,000 years.

Two thousand years ago, a distinction in language and culture between Siam and its neighbours occurred. The Siamese subsistence economy was based on the cultivation of rice, supplemented by fishing and the gathering of forest products. Trade in the area was conducted in commodities like pottery, metal tools and salt.

The country was sparsely populated. Villages were the centres of society and security, based on mutually-dependent trade in commodities such as salt and metal.

Rice-growing, forestry, metal products (particularly silver) and textiles can be traced back to these village times.

The Sukhothai Period (13th–15th Century)

People from Burma, Cambodia, and Laos moved into what is now Thailand nearly 1,000 years ago and founded a Khmer outpost at Sukhothai, which became the first capital of what was then called Siam. This is the first period of kingship recognised by the Thais, and lasted approximately from 1240 to 1450. In the last 100 years of this period, the power of Ayutthaya, a neighbouring city, challenged the Sukhothai regime.

Ramkamhaeng, the "Father of the People" and the third Sukhothai king, is said to have devised the Thai alphabet based on the Sanskrit alphabet. King Ramkamhaeng's evaluation of his reign and his kingdom is one of the cornerstones of the story of Thai prosperity.

The Ramkamhaeng Years

The king was benevolent and the land was prosperous. Trade was encouraged and crops were good. Everyone was well-fed and at peace. This period was regarded as the golden age of Thailand.

As King Ramkamhaeng himself declared about his own times and policies: "There is fish in the water and rice in the fields. The lord of the realm does not levy toll on his subjects for travelling…"

With varying degrees of success, the Sukhothai kings maintained bureaucratic and business control over much of central Siam until about 1430 when they were subsumed by the kingdom of the city of Ayutthaya, which then became the capital of Siam.

Ayutthaya Period (15th–17th Century)

By 1438, Ayutthaya was the undisputed centre of Siam; Buddhism was uniformly practised under Royal Decree and sanction. Siam became a nation of traders, controlled by royalty and Chinese merchants. These merchants, who traded primarily with China, had been invited to Ayutthaya.

Trade then, like today, was based on the export of agricultural and forest goods and the import of consumer products. Siam's major export commodity was rice and its major import was Chinese luxury goods.

Europeans were welcomed. As early as 1516, Siam signed a treaty with Portugal and later that century, Siam established trade agreements with the Netherlands, England, Spain and France.

Missionaries arrived to proselytise, giving the Siamese an opportunity to display to the world, the policy of passive resistance that had served the country well over the centuries. Both Islamic and Christian missionaries tried to influence the royal courts, and

Buddhism has been so infused into the lives of the Thais that in the Thai social hierarchy, even the king is subject to the Buddhist monks.

though both groups were allowed to practice their religion, neither of the outside religions was ever adopted by the kings. The Thais remained Buddhist despite centuries of efforts to persuade them into believing the superiority of a foreign god. It is this curious blend of apparent acceptance and actual rejection that has enabled Thailand to maintain its unique culture and ethos to this day.

In 1688, King Narai recognised the danger of French colonial ambitions and expelled the French. Trade with the Dutch and the Chinese continued, but the Siamese adopted a "divide and rule" policy with Europe. Siam is the only Southeast Asian nation that has never been colonised by a European power—a historical achievement of which the Thais are extremely proud. In fact, *Thailand*, the name chosen for Siam after the revolution of 1932, means "land of the free".

While successfully dealing with European colonial threat, Ayutthaya was twice attacked by the Burmese and once by the Cambodians. After the first attack, it quickly recovered and remained the religious and economic centre of Siam until the last of its 36 kings (King Suriyamarin) was ousted in the second Burmese attack in 1767.

Ayutthaya was then occupied by the Burmese, who remained there only six months before the city was recaptured by Siam's General Taksin. He subsequently declared himself king. Today, Ayutthaya is a collection of astonishing temple ruins which have been incorporated into the daily life of a flourishing country capital.

The Chakri Period (18th Century to Present Day)

The capital of Siam was moved from Ayutthaya to Thon Buri by General Taksin. However, it remained there for only 15 years before the first Chakri King moved it to the present site of Bangkok.

The Chakri period is divided into two periods: the absolute monarchy between 1782 and 1932 and the constitutional monarchy, which exists to the present day.

The first years of the Chakri dynasty were marked by extensive reform, and the utilisation of western technology and culture. It was not that the West was considered superior—Siam wanted to make itself acceptable to the West and thereby avoid conquest. In addition, the Siamese played off rival European countries against each other to avoid being colonised by the West, going so far as to give territory to both France and Britain.

King Rama I reopened trade with Europe, though he maintained a royal trade monopoly. Trade with China continued, and Chinese merchants and craftsmen were recruited to develop the local economy.

Rama II embarked on an ambitious programme of modernisation. His two major reforms laid the foundation for two of the main sources of trouble in Thailand today. In addition to changing social policies such as that of having to crawl before the king, he tried to implement a more efficient system of taxation by replacing tax farmers, who kept a percentage of the tax, with salaried tax collectors. He also reorganised the bureaucracy and the army. Men with education and good family backgrounds were employed in these two groups. The practice continued for many years. Today, these two groups have enormous influence on politics and business in Thailand.

By the time of Rama III in 1824, royal monopolies were abandoned and Siam was opened to free trade. The Treaty of Friendship and Commerce, also known as the Bowring Treaty, was negotiated with the United States and represented the closest that any Western power ever came to infringing on Siam's autonomy. It granted the United States the most favoured nation status and preferential tax treatment.

King Chulalongkorn or Rama V (1868–1910) made state visits abroad to observe modernisation and then embarked on an ambitious implementation of political and economic policies. For instance, governmental administration was enlarged and infrastructure was developed. To reinforce his military control, particularly in border areas, he organised a modern army along Western lines by establishing a Ministry of Defence, a king's guard regiment and a Military Cadet School. He also sent military officers for training abroad.

In addition, he sent his children to schools in Russia, Germany, Britain, France and England. The Western-educated princes then continued to mould governmental structure in accordance with European models. The Royal Court also hired foreign technicians and advisers with the relevant expertise to assist in the process of modernisation. This trend has continued to the present day—foreign advisers are still a part of life in Thailand.

During his reign, Siam became a major rice grower of the region, exporting rice particularly to India and China. The volume of rice exported increased between 1850 and 1900 from 60,000 tonnes of rice to 600,000 tonnes, while the price and amount of land in rice cultivation doubled. Such a considerable growth in the production of rice was achieved by the collective decisions of thousands of peasant families, who either cleared new land to expand the amount of land they cultivated or adopted more intensive methods of agriculture. In this period, Siam became and still is the only Asian country that is a net food exporter.

Siam declared its neutrality in the First World War, but subsequently turned against Germany when the United States entered the war. The Siamese deputation arrived on the battlefield at the end of the war, in time to view closing hostilities and participate in the victory. Siam was a signatory to the Treaty of Versailles and a founding member of the League of Nations, leading the way to modern Thailand's inclusion in trading alliances.

In 1920, the United States was the first country to give up its colonial aspirations in Siam. In fact, an American, Francis Sayers, was instrumental in helping Siam rid itself of all other foreign strongholds in the country. As a result of this historical event, Americans are still regarded as a favoured nation in Thailand today.

Although King Rama V's reforms helped Thailand resist colonisation, the formation of a powerful administration and a modern army, ironically, helped pave the way for the overthrow of the monarchy.

King Prajadhipok (Rama VII), the last absolute monarch of Thailand, lost his ruling powers to the military in 1932. Rama VII abdicated from the throne in 1935 to his ten-year-old nephew who was living in Switzerland at the time. No king resided in Thailand until 1950 when King Bhumibol Adulyadej (Rama IX), who still reigns today, brought his bride to Thailand where he was allowed to reign but not rule.

Under the constitution, the king was given executive and legislative powers through the parliament and the Council of Ministers. He was allowed to exercise judicial powers through the court of law. Theoretically, he had no political power and had to confine himself to a largely ceremonial role as head of state. In reality, however, the king plays a large role in maintaining stability in Thailand.

In the 1930s, the regime was geared towards dictatorship, characterised by the censorship of publications and radio speeches judged to be detrimental to public order. The formation of new political parties was prohibited. When Major Phibul Songkhram became prime minister in 1938, he embarked on an anti-Chinese and anti-Western campaign, calling himself "Leader" and ordering the Thai people to greet one another with the Hitler-like expression, "Hail Phibul".

Thailand adopted an ambivalent position during World War II, once more avoiding colonialism—by the Japanese this time—through passive resistance and ostensible cooperation. Knowing that occupation by Japan was inevitable, the country declared allegiance to the Axis cause and was occupied peacefully by Japan as a "protectionary force". At the end of the war, the United States again came to Thailand's rescue and persuaded the European powers into believing that Thailand had been coerced into the

Declaration of War. In 1946, Thailand was made the 55th signatory to the United Nations.

During the first half of the 20th century, Thailand's economy grew steadily and the country maintained its agricultural base. It was at this time that the movement toward labour-intensive manufacturing began.

Five Year Plans

The National Economic and Social Development Board (NESDB) was established in 1959 to coordinate and encourage five year economic plans. Its responsibility was to analyse and study economic and demographic data, and to create economic and social strategies that would help develop the Thai economy. Each plan had a different focus.

The 1960s

During the 1960s, the primary economic goal was import substitution. Thailand was primarily an agricultural economy then, based on the production and export of commodities such as rubber, rice, maize, sugar cane and seafood. However, the government decided to embark on an industrialisation programme to boost Thailand's economy.

Ironically, the instability of Thailand's neighbour, Vietnam, led to the resurgence of its fledgling tourism industry. During the 1960s, Thailand was the host country for American soldiers on recreational leave from the Vietnam War and the tourist industry began to develop in coastal towns, particularly Phuket and Pattaya.

The 1970s

The 1970s saw a democratic revolution in Thailand as the urban middle classes came to see the military's inability to deal with Thailand's economic problems. Student demonstrations in 1973 and 1976 brought the downfall of military rule.

In the meantime, the industrialisation programme began in the 1960s continued. Consumer goods made up the bulk of the manufacturing industry. The manufacture of capital goods and more advanced and sophisticated products such as pharmaceuticals and chemicals had not yet started. Thailand recognised the nations of China in 1975 and Vietnam in 1976, showing its awareness of developing economies in the region.

The 1980s
In the 1980s, Thailand pursued a social agenda aimed at equalising income. During this period, Thailand developed a significant domestic consumer economy as the per capita income rose. Policies were introduced to upgrade infrastructure, control pollution and population, decentralise production, and diversify the industry base. These policies have yet to be thoroughly implemented. It was also in this period that Thailand's economy benefited from a surge of Japanese investment money, which was concentrated in property development.

The 1990s
In 1991, the military took over again in a bloodless coup—the 17th coup in Thailand's short constitutional history. The episode capped a continuing drive towards a firmer degree of civilian democracy in Thailand in the past decade, riding on the back of impressive economic growth.

After almost four decades of industrial development, Thailand derived 42% of its GDP from the industrial sector. The Pacific Rim emerged as an economic force in the closing years of the 1980s and the first half of the 1990s.

During the 1990s, Thailand's economy ran into constraints. Other countries in the region were growing rapidly and Thailand experienced competition from nations in the region such as China, Vietnam and Bangladesh. These countries, like Thailand, were beginning to industrialise from an agrarian base. They, however,

Thailand's Competitiveness

In 1996, Thailand slipped from the 14th to the 18th place in the annual global competitiveness ranking by the World Economic Forum, based on a survey of 58 countries by journalists and executives working in various countries. The Forum also singled out 10 countries whose governments had worsened their countries' competitiveness in the past year. The Thai Government was ranked third.

The IMF survey of competitiveness placed Thailand at number 28 of 46 countries surveyed. This is a more plausible ranking in terms of current restraints and is likely to drop further still as the full effects of IMF policies are felt.

have significantly lower labour costs than Thailand, so competition was most felt in low-skill industry sectors such as textile, footwear and clothing—the mainstays of the intensive labour export component of the Thai economy.

Competition also grew from the newly emerging Eastern European bloc countries such as the Czech Republic. The market share of Thai goods in the United States declined because higher Thai labour costs increased the cost of textiles, footwear, toys and sports equipment in relation to other NICs in the region. In addition, export items from Thailand were conceived to be of poorer quality than those from the other NICs.

Thai industry resisted the adoption of modern methods of doing business, so its technology and skills base remained stagnant and outdated. Government scandals and frequent changes in government also decreased overseas confidence in Thailand's ability to consistently produce items of good quality.

In 1996, the overheated economy ran into a period of retraction caused by constraints in resources. The Securities Exchange of Thailand (SET) index on the stock exchange experienced a dramatic slump when the market in general lost its

Thailand: A Statistical Overview

Area	514,000 sq km
Land Boundaries	Laos, Myanmar, Cambodia, Malaysia
Coastline	1,840 km on Gulf of Thailand, 865 km on Indian Ocean
Terrain	flat central plain, mountains in north-east and along the western border
Land Use	26% forest
Population	60 million
Population Growth	1.4%
Birth Rate	1.3%
Life Expectancy	67 for women, 64 for men
Language	Thai, Chinese
Literacy	Under 30 years old (100%); over 30 (uncertain)
Ethnic Divisions	Thai, Chinese
Religion	Buddhism (95%), Muslim (3%), Hindu/Christian (2%)
Electric Current	220 volts, 50 cycles AC
Currency	Baht
Major Cities	Bangkok, Chiang Mai, Phuket, Pattaya
Major Imports	Capital goods (44%), intermediate products (28%), consumer goods (11%), others (17%)
Major Exports	Manufactured goods (81%), agricultural products (11%), fishery products (6%), others (2%)
GDP per capita	60,000 baht (1996)
Time	GMT plus 7 hours
Fiscal Year	1 July–30 June

nerve and foreign investors cashed in their investments. This slump was followed by a severe downturn on the SET in 1997.

Government Economic Policy

Governments change but the Thai *laissez faire* attitude to business does not. The government presently controls a large percentage of the public infrastructure through 65 state enterprises, though privatisation is increasing in telecommunications, transportation and other sectors. Manufacturing and construction, the fastest growing sectors of the economy in recent years, have the highest degree of foreign ownership.

Government Economic Objectives
In 1996, the Senate Committee stated that the government should aim to:

- Tighten monetary and fiscal policies—the current policy with a ratio of 70% monetary and 30% fiscal will be reversed (this statement indicates an intention to raise taxes, which are low by international standards)
- Manage foreign debts prudently
- Closely monitor the basket of currencies system
- Maintain the stability of financial institutions
- Privatise the energy market
- Implement consumer price control
- Promote investment in export-oriented businesses
- Improve the efficiency of the agricultural sector

Whether any of these pronouncements find their way into actual policies has yet to be determined. It is certain that the International Monetary Fund (IMF), which intervened in August 1997 with emergency funding for the battered economy, will demand the implementation of these measures.

Monetary and Fiscal Policy

Monetary policy is set by the Bank of Thailand (BOT) and a belated attempt is being made to restrain credit growth while keeping interest rates high. The difference between local and overseas interest rates encouraged companies to turn to foreign capital until the baht was floated in 1997, which accounted for the high rate of private debts in Thailand.

Fiscal policy includes government expenditure, public revenues, fiscal reserves and public debt management.

Government expenditure is relatively low compared to GNP (estimated at between 16% and 19%) because public sector involvement is limited to providing a framework for the economy's regulation and expansion. The budget reflects these priorities.

Government Expenditure (US$billion)

Year	Revenues	Expenses	Surplus	% GDP
1991	18.1	14.1	3.0	4.0
1992	21.6	17.7	3.9	2.4
1993	22.6	20.5	2.0	1.7
1994	27.0	23.0	4.0	2.8
1995	31.1	25.1	6.0	3.3

Source: Office of the Prime Minister statistics

The surplus indicated in the table above disappeared in 1996 and by July 1997, government spending was in deficit. Fiscal reserves plunged.

Public revenue in 1996 came from taxes (55%), excise (20%), customs (15%), state enterprises (5%) and other agencies (5%). As unemployment rises, taxes will decrease and revenue will drop.

In 1996, community and social services accounted for 41% of expenditure, over half of which was allocated to education, followed by public health. Economic expenditure accounted for 28% of expenditure, over half of which was allocated to transport and communication. The remaining 31% went to administration, principally to defence.

A cautious monetary and fiscal policy will be in place in Thailand for some years. Priority will remain with developing industry, supporting business and encouraging foreign investment.

The Organised Financial Market

The legal Thai finance market includes 15 commercial banks, 33 finance houses, agricultural cooperatives, savings cooperatives, life insurance companies and credit financiers. As of November 1997, trading in another 58 institutions was suspended indefinitely and only two have been allowed to reopen.

Specialised financial institutions have been created by the government to deal with specific problems, one institution in each sector. Among these institutions are the Government Savings Bank, the Bank of Agriculture and Agricultural Cooperatives, the Industrial Finance Corporation of Thailand, the Government Housing Bank and the Export Import Bank of Thailand.

The business community obtains about 72% of its finance from commercial banks and about 18% is borrowed from finance companies, with other institutions supplying the remaining 10%.

The Commercial Banking Act of 1979 attempted to control the policies of commercial banks by directing investment into selected sectors. In 1997, 56 financial institutions which failed to implement the suggestions of the act were investigated.

By 1993, there were 15 local commercial banking firms—including 14 foreign banks—with 2,700 branches in Thailand. About one-fifth of these banks were in Bangkok, although the network spreads to most upcountry towns.

In 1996 and 1997, the banks came under pressure as the property values and stock prices of the overheated economy crumbled. Several of the biggest banks received government help when it became evident that the paper assets and real assets of the banks were not the same

The government's 1997 bailout package of the troubled banking industry was controversial. The banking industry's critics, believing that the industry was responsible for causing its own problems in the first place by imprudent lending practices, thought that the banks were let off much too easily at the taxpayers' expense. Many Thais (especially civil servants) fear the government will draw on public savings pools such as the civil service pension system to help bail out the sagging property sector. Savings from government employees currently amount to about 15% of the country's monetary base.

Historically, foreign banks have not been welcome in Thailand. In response to the current situation, this policy is changing. Overseas competition could improve the efficiency of Thai banks but can do little to improve the existing situation.

Further, a decision was recently made to grant licences to 12 life assurance companies and 16 general insurers, the first time such licences have been granted in 15 years. So far, only local companies have participated in the scheme.

Whose Fault Was It?

In its role in bailing out the financial sector and unsuccessfully attempting to defend the baht against the raid by currency speculators in the financial crisis of 1996/97, the Bank of Thailand was singled out for criticism. In July 1997, such pressures led to the resignation of the chairman of the bank, Mr. Rernchai Marakanond. However, most financial commentators feel that the Bank of Thailand was merely a scapegoat for the government's ineptitude. They believed that the country's problems were caused by more deep-seated issues like government corruption, the failure of the government to salvage the economy despite early warning signs and the lack of requisite leadership.

The Bank of Thailand

The Bank of Thailand, established in 1942, acts as the country's central bank. Its main branch is in Bangkok but it also maintains offices in Songkla and Lampang.

It issues notes and acts as a banker to the government. It is also the lender of last resort for local commercial banks. It is the agency which handles international monetary funds for the government, manages public debt and maintains exchange rates and policy. It supervises the Securities Exchange of Thailand (SET) and creates policy for and manages commercial banks and other sources of public credit. In addition, its research and public information department is an excellent source of financial data, coordinating Thailand's drive to become the banking centre of the Southeast Asian region.

The currency of Thailand is called the "baht", where the "satang" is the minor unit at one hundredth of a baht. Since the baht has a low value, the satang is no longer widely circulated and has only nuisance value. Coinage covers currency denominations of up to 10 baht, with notes of incremental value from 20 baht to 1,000 baht in circulation. Plastic bank notes are being introduced and are being purchased from Australia, a world leader in the manufacture of plastic currency.

Until recently, the value of the baht was set daily by the board of the Bank of Thailand. For many years, the exchange rate between the Thai baht and the US dollar was stabilised at about 25 baht to one US dollar.

However in 1997, with the erosion of the national debt position, currency speculators mounted an attack on the baht, plunging its value to below 40 baht to the US dollar in November 1997. For a few months, the Bank of Thailand supported the baht against speculators, buying it aggressively. It is estimated that US$23.4 billion was used to defend the baht.

In early July 1997, the Bank of Thailand floated the baht, leaving it to find its own level in the marketplace. The chairman of the Bank of Thailand resigned his position a few weeks later, followed closely by the finance minister.

It was believed that if the baht could maintain an exchange value of about 35 baht to the US dollar, Thailand could recover quickly. A favourite bar game in Bangkok is guessing what the baht will be worth in late 1998. The reality is that no country can predict the direction of its currency until it comes to terms with the global economy, a lesson that Thailand is learning.

Two new structures, the Financial Restructuring Authority and the Asset Management Corporation, were created in 1997 to deal with the problems of the 58 financial institutions under threat.

The Securities Exchange of Thailand (SET)

Established in 1974, the SET is, in theory, closely monitored by the Bank of Thailand and the Office of the Securities and Exchange Commission (SEC).

In 1993, there were 347 companies listed on the SET. The volume of trade conducted on the exchange expanded rapidly in the early period of its establishment. In the early 1990s, when the SET index was rising strongly, investing in Thai stock became popular with offshore investors. The absence of capital gains tax and favourable tax treatment of dividends from listed companies made investment attractive.

The market reached its highest point towards the end of 1993, when it climbed to 1,800 points. In the roller coaster economy of the 1990s, the second half of 1997 revealed the SET index to be at about 500 points, a value lower than that of a decade before. It is also a massive decline of 70% from its all-time high value.

For those who fancy investing in the Thai market, a few conditions apply. Foreigners with work permits are entitled to invest. However, as is usual for most things in Thailand, a heap of registration paperwork is required, including the submission of several copies of your passport, work permit, bank statement of the last six months and "other (unspecified) related documents".

Assuming the documentation is approved, you must then pay a minimum of 500,000 baht to secure an opening portfolio.

In general, foreigners with a passion to invest in Thailand in a hassle-free way, should enlist the help of a foreign-owned unit trust. Foreigners in a hurry to repatriate their earnings should think twice about investing at all.

Inflation and Gross National Product (GNP)

The remarkable economic growth rate of the 1990s has put some pressure on prices. As such, inflation has been higher in Thailand than its major trading partners.

Along with the Asian Tigers, Thailand enjoyed growth rates of over 10% per year throughout the 1980s. In the early 1990s, a growth rate of over 8% was recorded. However, the growth rate has slowed down dramatically in 1996 and the predicted growth rate for 1997 is between 1.5%–3%. It is not expected to pick up until mid-1998 or later.

Gross National Product

Year	GDP (US$billion)	Annual Increase of GDP (%)	GDP per capita
1991	112.7	8.5	1978
1992	121.8	8.1	2137
1993	131.9	8.3	2261
1994	143.5	8.8	2430
1995	156.0	8.7	2624
1996	166.4	6.7	2773
1997	176.2	1.5–3	2937

Source: National Economic and Social Development Board

Note:
1. All figures are at constant 1994 prices.
2. Figures for 1997 are estimated.

Major Sectors

After 30 years of industrial development, manufacturing is now the biggest sector of the Thai economy. The biggest single industry is tourism, which is spread across various sectors, including retail trading, transportation and other services.

Gross National Product by Industry

	Percentage of GNP
Manufacture	28.2
Wholesale and Retail Trade	16.4
Services	12.6
Agriculture	10.2
Banking, Insurance and Real Estate	7.9
Transport and Communication	7.5
Construction	7.4
Public Administration and Defence	3.5
Ownership of Dwellings	2.5
Electricity and Water Supply	2.3
Mining and Quarrying	1.4
Total	100.0

Source: *Pocket Thailand in Figures*, 1996

The structure of the Thai industry has shifted from more resource-intensive activities such as food, beverages and tobacco to labour-intensive activities. The next stage of development will most likely be in capital-intensive industries like chemicals, paper products, transport and iron and steel, and the emerging high-technology products such as chemicals, office equipment and scientific equipment.

The development of service industries such as shipping, banking, insurance and tourism are likely to be important. Since the service sector is the fastest growing area of the global economy, its development presents the country with the greatest opportunity to earn precious foreign exchange dollars. At present, most of the shipping charges find their way overseas, due mainly to Thailand's lack of international involvement in this field.

Major Trading Partners

Although Thailand is a founder member of ASEAN, the main trading bloc of the region, the total contribution of all ASEAN countries to Thai exports and imports in 1995 was only 18% and 13% respectively. Thailand's major trading partners and regions fall outside its immediate geographical area.

Thailand's Major Trading Partners, 1994

Exports (Value in $ Billion)		Imports (Value in $ Billion)	
Country	% Total	Country	% Total
USA	20.8	Japan	30.2
Japan	17.2	USA	11.8
Singapore	13.7	Singapore	6.3
Hong Kong	5.3	Germany	5.9
Germany	3.5	Taiwan	5.1
United Kingdom	3.0	Malaysia	4.9
Netherlands	2.8	South Korea	3.6
Malaysia	2.4	China	2.6
Taiwan	2.2	United Kingdom	2.1
China	2.1	Australia	2.0

Thailand currently enjoys Generalised System of Preferences (GSP) status with the United States, the country's largest export destination. GSP preferences are extended to countries with a low per capita income. In this scheme, a ceiling of $8,600 per annum is put on GSP status. Thailand does not seem likely to reach this ceiling in the near future.

Exports and Imports by Product

Tourism is Thailand's biggest earner of foreign exchange dollars. The export pattern of other products is diversified and is spread over labour-intensive manufacture and agricultural commodities.

Like most growing NICs, Thailand imports capital equipment and hi-tech consumer goods. It also imports oil, though not as much as it used to in the 1980s.

Import and Export by Product, 1994

Imports		Exports	
Product Class	Percentage	Product Class	Percentage
Electrical Equipment	18.7	Tourism	12.6
Mechanical Equipment	18.7	Computer Parts	7.5
Vehicles	7.9	Textiles	7.4
Iron and Steel	6.8	Rubber	4.4
Petroleum Products	6.8	Integrated Circuits	4.2
Plastics	3.7	Footwear	3.9
Chemicals	3.3	Plastic Products	3.8
Precious Stones	2.5	Gems and Jewellery	3.8
Steel Parts	2.3	Frozen Seafood	3.7
Scientific Instruments	1.9	Rice	3.5

Source: *Pocket Thailand in Figures*, 1996

Farm products include maize, tobacco, rubber, processed chicken, frozen vegetable and fruit, rice, coffee and tapioca. Agricultural industry products include canned seafood, rubber products, canned fruit and vegetables, rice products and animal feed, as well as sugar.

One of Thailand's economic strengths is the diverse nature of its economy. This diversity shows up in both exports and domestic production. According to the table above, the top ten exports by value account for less than 50% of the total value of all exports.

External Trading Account

In the early 1990s, the high economic growth rate and the growing consumer economy attracted large volumes of capital and consumer imports. To counteract the import imbalance, the country earns net foreign exchange through its services sector, in particular tourism.

However, tourism earnings have not been sufficient to cover the difference between the import and export of physical goods. Therefore, the Thai economy has run a persistent current account deficit of over 7% of the GDP throughout the 1990s. In 1997 this problem had not been fully addressed. Accumulated foreign debt resulting from the unending series of current account deficits has put pressure on other aspects of the economy, in particular the exchange rate.

Foreign Investment in Thailand

Notwithstanding the economic hiccup of the mid-1990s, the growth of long-term foreign investment in Thailand has been vigorous. The strongest area of economic growth has been in the consumer goods industry, both for domestic consumption and export. This is a direct result of the country's long-term industrialisation programmes.

Government policy aims to encourage both local and foreign investment. To promote this policy, the government (through its investment arm, the Board of Investment (BOI)), offers special promotional privilege for companies setting up factories in Thailand. In 1995, about 1,000 companies established industrial facilities under the BOI investment programme.

Foreign investors are attracted to Thailand rather than some of the neighbouring countries such as Cambodia, Laos, Burma and Vietnam because of its more highly developed infrastructure, higher workforce skills and relative political stability. Japanese investors who initiated the Thai economic boom of the 1980s are expected to continue locating production facilities in Thailand, assuming costs remain stable and labour productivity continues to increase.

Foreign Debt

The series of persistent current account deficits in the 1980s and 1990s have been financed by overseas borrowing and foreign equity investment. As a result, net overseas debt (the difference between money lent to and invested in Thailand by foreigners, and money lent and invested by Thais in other countries) has increased over the years. Most of the foreign debt is generated by the private sector.

Overseas debt, a problem faced by many countries in the world, creates a future interest bill that must be serviced either by export earnings or by further borrowings. Mounting debt was one of the factors that alarmed stock market investors in mid-1996. In 1997, it pushed the SET index down to a ten-year low and put the skids under the baht. Net Indebtedness has more than doubled in five years, rising from 30% to 54% of the GNP.

The International Monetary Fund (IMF)

As the foreign indebtedness of Thailand increases, the country will fall under the influence of foreign managers and bankers, such as the IMF. This is a fate that many countries, such as those in Latin America and Eastern Europe, have already suffered in the past 30 years. The Latin American experience has been that, when indebtedness passes certain debt service ratios, the extension of further credit puts the indebted country at the funding agency's mercy, so to speak.

The IMF procedure dictates that the country do things the IMF way. It includes, in particular, the obligations to provide government services in a transparent way, to manage the economy well and to tackle hard economic issues head-on.

It is fair to say that some of these methods are in conflict with deeply-ingrained Thai culture and ways of doing business.

The $17.2 billion bailout carries with it the following conditions and targets for Thailand's growth.

IMF Targets	1997	1998	1999–2000
GDP growth %	2.5	3.5	6–7.0
Inflation %	9.5	5.0	4–5
current account %	-5.0	-3.0	-3 to -4
foreign reserves $b	23.0	24.5	30.0
fiscal balance % GDP	-1.1	1.0	1–2
money supply	7.0	11.0	12–15
foreign debt/GDP	55.5	59.6	55–60

Summary

The following table of economic indicators was compiled by Asiarisk. The figures for 1997 will show a sharp drop in GDP, a decrease in exports, a decrease in imports, a bigger current account deficit, hardly any foreign reserves, increased long term debt and a much higher exchange rate.

Economic Indicators	1991	1992	1993	1994	1995	1996
Real GDP growth (%)	7.89	7.40	7.80	8.80	8.60	6.70
Total exports	28.44	32.47	36.78	45.13	56.46	55.81
Total imports	37.58	40.68	45.92	54.46	70.78	72.44
Current account balance	7.57	-6.36	-6.36	-8.09	-13.55	-14.70
Foreign exchange reserves	17.29	20.01	24.08	28.88	35.46	38.70
Total long-term external debt	25.61	24.89	26.10	31.81	33.49	39.50
Exchange rate vs US$ (year-end)	25.28	25.52	25.54	25.09	25.16	25.61
Inflation (CPI %)	5.72	4.10	3.40	5.20	5.70	5.90

The Thai economy prospered on trade based on agricultural products for a long time. In the later half of the century, manufactured goods took precedence. It then experienced a period of unprecedented growth based on an influx of foreign capital and property development. However, Thailand is experiencing difficulties as it tries to compete on the manufacturing market without the efficiency, productivity and quality control of the industrialised nations. Thailand needs more expertise in the engineering, computer and marketing fields to compete effectively with Hong Kong, Malaysia and Singapore.

Government reaction to the 1997 downturn is inconsistent. It is not certain if and how the government will tackle the persistent problems encountered by foreign investors such as the Alien Business Law, work permit regulations, long waits for value added tax refunds, and poor customs laws and procedures. After all, such complaints have been unheeded for 20 years.

Cultural habits die hard. Thais do not tackle issues head-on. They are neither good at conflict resolution nor are they very disciplined. One of the more charming Thai philosophies is *mai pen rai*, meaning "never mind". Although such a philosophy works well in most aspects of life, it can have negative effects in business. This state of mind is similar to the Arabic *Inshallah* and the Latin *manana*. In short, since things may get better tomorrow, one should give the future time to work itself out.

As the early 1990s roared along to seemingly effortless prosperity—indeed the boom was not expected to end—there was some build-up of an infallibility complex. For the first few years of the 1990s, Thai business believed itself to be the all-conquering Asian Tiger of the world economy. Recently, there has been a fall to reality and a period of introspection.

By and large, Thai managers are not good at paying attention to detail. They are the original "broad picture" people—often, this broad picture is fairly fuzzy. As a result of the recent crisis, Thai managers will have to make an adjustment from the boom mentality to a more professional and competitive approach to business The Thai Government will have to adjust its goals to comply with IMF demands and at the same time, try to maintain national independence. If there is any nation that can manage both goals, Thailand can. After all, Thailand seems to have been able to obtain foreign help without foreign domination better than almost any other nation—if its history is any indication.

Long time investors of Thailand say they have maintained or improved their business positions during past crises. The present crisis may, in a way, also provide the new investor with business opportunities. Some of these are described in the following chapter.

CHAPTER 4

Business Opportunities

This chapter contains guidelines on how to make contact with the relevant departments and people for important information on the type of business chosen. It also gives tips on the completion of necessary paperwork before business proper. In addition, this chapter provides an overview of economic sectors in Thailand.

Making Contact

The Board of Investment (BOI) is the government agency whose main responsibility is to encourage you, the foreign investor, to come to Thailand. The BOI operates extensively through Thai embassies outside Thailand, providing useful information regarding investment in Thailand, including the rules and regulations governing it. If you are without a contact for your putative business operation in Thailand, the local embassy is one place to start. The Thai Trade Association is active all over the world and can help you get current BOI information. A list of offices around the world is included in Appendix B.

Working with, but independent from, the BOI is the Industrial Estates Authority of Thailand (IEAT), whose authority encompasses most of the initial setup activities of an investor, manufacturer or importer. The IEAT will undertake feasibility studies, acquire and develop land, invest in infrastructure, sell or lease developed land, and provide support services and facilities to industrialists within the states. They will also do market research and evaluate foreign investors' proposals before formal presentation to government agencies. Making contact with them is useful once you have chosen the business in which you want to invest, particularly if you want to build a plant.

There are many business networks such as chambers of commerce, business associations and expatriate organisations, which will provide assistance to foreign business people. Thais have a well-deserved reputation for friendliness and are curious about outsiders. It is easy to strike up an acquaintanceship with a Thai at a meeting or a social event. Thai business people network very extensively, so you will benefit by getting involved in whatever local organisations are appropriate to your business.

Make business cards for yourself as soon as you reach Thailand—English on one side, Thai on the other. Distribute your card widely. Thais are great hoarders of business cards and tend to produce theirs at every opportunity.

Feasibility Studies

Thais tend to have an optimistic approach to life. When embarking on projects, they tend to assume that everything will turn out for the best. This attitude is a result of the *my pen rai* philosophy. As such, they may sometimes have an unrealistic opinion of the outcome of the intended project. If you are a potential joint venture partner in a project in Thailand, the onus will most likely be on you to check out the local market, even though your Thai partner is in a much better position to do so. He or she will likely assume that all will be well in the end.

A point that should be mentioned to those from developed countries is that it is easy to become convinced that because labour costs are cheaper in Thailand than in your home country, the overall project costs will also be less. This is a message peddled by financial journalists in many countries, in articles touting the need to reduce labour costs at home.

The cost advantage of setting up businesses in countries like Thailand can be greatly exaggerated. Labour costs will certainly be less. However, the cost of materials and the cost of utilities such as electricity may be higher. Rents and building costs may also be rather expensive. Though labour costs may be lower, labour productivity, labour skills and attitudes to quality may also not be as high.

Two opposing trends should be considered when you evaluate the Thai market size for your product. One is that Thais tend to resist buying local goods because they think they are substandard. The other is the current "buy Thai" campaign that stresses the importance of supporting local industry.

Made in Thailand

In 1993, an Australian manufacturer and a Thai partner established a factory for the manufacture of aluminium petrol tankers for sale to the Thai oil industry. After the first prototype was built, it was found that buyers in the Thai market were resistant to products made in Thailand because they believed the competitive product imported from the United States would be superior due to its country of origin. Also, since Australia was not considered a technologically-developed country in Thailand, the Australian design was considered suspect.

As a consequence, in order to produce sales on the Thai market, the Thai-made Australian-designed product had to be priced 30% lower than the equivalent American import.

Market Research

A few years ago, little market research was carried out in Thailand. At the time, the country was an expanding economy with apparently limitless demand. Today, however, more importers, manufacturers and wholesalers are using market research. This trend is likely to continue.

IEAT facilities with advice on market sizes and shares are widely available. If independent advice is required, market research consultants are listed in the English Bangkok phone directory. The BOI also provides information on the size of some markets, as does the Bureau of Statistics. If your Thai business partner assures you that she/he knows the market, it is best to confirm the data from an independent source. It is easy to misjudge the demand for any good or service in a market that is changing as rapidly as Thailand's and in a culture as unfamiliar as the Thais'.

Other sources of market research include the Thailand Productivity Institute, which was formed in 1994 under the Ministry of Industry. You can also check the Internet for specific industry surveys and if you are in Bangkok, DK Books in Seacon Square—a shopping mall in Bangkok—has a good selection of books on import and export markets, and business statistics.

Imports

Opportunities for Importers

Thailand's high import tariffs and arbitrary customs valuation procedures have constituted significant barriers to trade with the country. However, since 1994, in compliance with the General Agreement on Trade and Tariffs (GATT) Uruguay Round commitments, Thailand has embarked on a trade policy which concentrates on a continuous programme of tariff reduction on imported goods. The objective of such a policy is the eventual reduction of tariffs to between 0% and 5% on all goods by the year 2003. Different tariff rates apply to different goods. Information on specific tariff categories can be obtained from the Customs Department.

Imports required in Thailand include raw materials that can be processed cheaply, capital equipment, and luxury or specialty items not available in Thailand. You could also regard your business acumen or expertise as an import commodity if you are able to act as a consultant or adviser in a developing sector in Thailand.

Import Agents

New market entrants should appoint an established agent/ distributor with technical expertise in the specific field, who also has good contacts in and knowledge of the local market. Reputable local consultants are usually qualified to design market-entry strategies and to locate suitable partners. Begin with your embassy or go to the English Yellow Pages if you are not certain about who to talk to or how to meet consultants. If you are already in Thailand, you may have already met suitably qualified people through your personal network.

Use your fax or e-mail rather than the phone when you are establishing contact. Most Thais are much better at reading English than speaking it. Firms exporting goods and services should invest time in selecting qualified agents to market their products and services, and should allow sufficient budgets for staff training, marketing and technical support staff.

There are three basic types of importers that act as agents or distributors. The first category includes large, well-established trading companies with strong financial resources, large sales volumes and extensive commercial presence in multiple industry sectors. This category includes major Japanese trading companies, the Thai-owned Berli Juker, the US-owned Louis T. Leonowens, and European-based trading companies like B. Grimm, Diethelm, East Asiatic Company, FE Zuellig and Inchcape.

In certain specialised sub-sectors of the market, these large import/distribution companies use sub-dealers or agents to help them concentrate their efforts. This is the case, for example, in the defence industry where personal relationships are very important. These large firms often propose marketing or production joint ventures when imports to Thailand reach a level sufficient for the justification of local investment.

The second category of importers include agents and distributors who generally specialise in one line of business in which they have well-established contacts and market knowledge.

The third category represents small companies expanding into the import and distribution business. Many of these companies import goods that cater to the expatriate community.

Frequent contact is important, especially at the outset of the venture, to build a good working relationship with all partners. This also ensures that the exporter and local agent are pursuing common goals. Product information and training are essential.

Personal Importing

Alternatively, especially for a small venture, you may wish to establish your own import company within Thailand. You will then be subject to Thai rules of company incorporation. An importer who is not a Thai citizen is regarded as an alien, whose participation in Thai business is governed by the Alien Business Law. Such importers may face many restrictions and licensing regulations. The guiding principle is that anything that can be easily produced in Thailand will most likely be rejected for importation. This principle is applied to imports that are processed and then re-exported, as well as to products for consumption within the kingdom itself.

Do bear in mind that a Certificate of Payment from the Bank of Thailand or another authorised bank is required before the Customs Department clears imported goods. A substantial oiling of the wheels may be necessary to get the right paperwork issued. The hidden and unpredictable costs of getting goods released from customs are the main difficulties of importing goods into Thailand.

Personal Marketing

You could also set up a direct marketing company for imports in Thailand. Thais view direct marketing as an excellent way to expand their social and business networks. Direct marketing is a growing industry and is already used extensively to sell household wares, cosmetics and car care products.

This industry is largely unregulated and a direct marketing company is easy to set up. All you have to do is rent a space, acquire telephone lines, register the company with the Commercial

Registration Department and declare the imported goods you intend to sell. The government is currently investigating the types of controls that are needed to prevent fraudulent practices.

Franchise

Many leading international fast food franchises are established in Thailand. However, smaller franchises also exist in other sectors. Thais are increasingly receptive to franchising, both as customers and partners. Thai incomes rose rapidly in the early 1990s ($6,000 per capita GNP in Bangkok) and there was a strong preference for popular Western brands. When the economy recovers from the 1997 currency crisis, those franchises in place will be in a position to take advantage of the revived economy.

The best way for a franchiser to enter the market is through involvement with a Thai joint venture partner. The joint venture should be so structured as to allow the overseas franchisers to retain majority control, as well as to ensure uniformity with their established working system. A joint venture will also be more acceptable to franchisees since they will be dealing with people of their own nationality.

Good prospects for franchising are automotive services educational and technical training, as well as maintenance and cleaning operations.

Domestic Attitudes to Imported Goods

Most Thais regard goods from other countries as meeting quality standards lacking in their own country. Goods from Japan, Germany and the United States are perceived to be of high quality. Goods from the rest of Europe rank next, while goods from Korea and Taiwan are perceived to have improving quality. On the other hand, goods from places like Africa, South America and Australia are not very well-known in the marketplace and may be overlooked if similar goods are available from the countries of perceived high quality or status.

Luxury goods like fine wine, perfume and designer clothes are much valued. The amount spent on imported personal items and clothes, for instance, rose by more than 500% between 1981 and 1996. Labels are very important. Taxes are increasing on such goods but they are still regarded as desirable status symbols.

Exports

The government aims to promote exports through value added tax rebates and numerous investment incentives.

There are only two restrictions on the export of goods from Thailand. Firstly, there must be an adequate supply of staples, such as rice and sugar for local consumption. Secondly, Thai product quality and export management standards must be met.

Governing local exports are the Export Standard Act (No 2) and the Controlling Importation and Exportation of Goods Act, both passed in 1979 and in need of revision. The acts are administered by the Commodity Standards Office of the Ministry of Commerce. Aliens must also follow the regulations of Alien Business Law. See chapter five for the regulations and incentives of establishing an export business.

Export Finance and Insurance

Banks in Thailand are anxious to obtain foreign customers. The specialist bank for exports is the Export-Import Bank of Thailand in Klongtoey. In addition, most overseas banks have offices in Bangkok. A list of banks is included in Appendix B.

Specific Market Segments

Opportunities for large scale investment can be found in manufacture, specifically of automobile and computer parts, and in infrastructure, particularly energy and transportation. Government projects are also a possibility.

Short-term or medium-sized investment will most likely be in services like tourism and education, or in import and export.

A list of BOI investment categories is available from the BOI and changes yearly. It is a good reference tool to identify the market segments in which you may be interested in investing. Take note of sectors in which foreigners are encouraged to invest or prohibited from doing so.

Tourism

Tourism is the single most important foreign currency earner in the Thai economy. It is also the single most important industry in the country. Tourism has been Thailand's highest income generator since 1982, having grown about 16% annually since 1980. In 1994, visitor arrivals reached a record 6.6 million. The rate of growth of tourism is the highest in Asia, with the visitor rate from Hong Kong growing the fastest.

Tourism in Thailand, 1994

Originating Country	Percentage of Tourists
Malaysia	14.6
Japan	15.1
Taiwan	7.3
Singapore	6.3
South Korea	6.0
Germany	5.7
Hong Kong	5.0
USA	4.7
United Kingdom	4.3
China	4.2

Source: *Pocket Thailand in Figures*

The biggest tourist area outside Bangkok is Pattaya in the province of Chon Buri. This centre was and still is, an "R&R" centre for the US navy. Over the years, a resort has developed without central planning. Today, the resort itself and some of the less

The elephant shows in Chiang Mai draw in many tourists every year.

reputable street life aspects of Pattaya have attracted censure from both Thais and overseas tourists.

Other major tourist destinations include the beaches of Phuket to the south and the mountains of Chiang Mai and Chiang Rai to the north. Phuket is in the process of being upgraded to an international duty free centre to rival that of Singapore.

The Tourism Authority of Thailand (TAT)—the major government body that controls tourism—acts in conjunction with the BOI to develop facilities, particularly in the provinces. The TAT periodically reviews policy in regard to the promotion of investment in tourist-related facilities, such as hotels and regional attractions. TAT has adopted the phrase "Amazing Thailand" as the theme of its 1998–1999 tourism campaign.

Thailand has begun coordinating tourism activities in the surrounding regions. On 1 January 1997, the Tourism Authority of Thailand (TAT) became the official coordinator for all tourism projects in the Greater Mekong sub-region. As infrastructure improves and visa requirements are simplified, travel through the region will become easier and tourism should increase rapidly.

Many reasons can be attributed to the growth of Thailand as an attractive tourist destination. Since the 1997 baht devaluation, it has the additional advantage, so far as tourists are concerned, of being one of the cheapest destinations in Southeast Asia.

Factors that Promote Tourism in Thailand

- Attractive appearance and manners of the Thai people
- Removal of the AIDS stigma
- Strong product development
- Business travel and conventions
- Relaxed airline policies
- Cooperation between Thai Airways International and global alliance partners
- Value for money
- TAT promotions
- Provincial airline developments
- Increasing involvement of universities and colleges

Tourism has been successful in the past because the Thais have always extended a warm welcome to strangers. However, like many countries experiencing tourist fatigue, some less than favourable practices have emerged that need to be examined. The industry is conscious of the need to resist victimisation of tourists. Examples include taxi drivers at the airport and tourist destinations, who can alienate tourists. The two-tier system of pricing in Thailand, where tourists may pay up to two to three times the local price for the same goods, may also anger them. You, as a temporary resident, can avoid the more extreme examples of exploitation by pleasantly telling the driver or tradesperson that you live in Thailand.

Over the years, Thailand has also acquired a negative image as a tourist destination. Potential tour operators may need to dispel such concerns in the mind of the tourist.

Negative Aspects of Thailand

- Environmental issues
- Bangkok traffic
- Organised crime
- Touts
- Problems with Thai Airways International
- Bureaucracy
- Technological deficiencies in telecommunications
- Weakness of tourist associations

TAT conducts periodic purges to improve the negative image of Thai tourism. Raids are often conducted on the Patpong area of Bangkok, (in)famous for its brothels and on hotels that do not have proper fire escape procedures and exits. However, some programmes backfire, such as littering fines, which have been applied almost exclusively to tourists, while others prove to be only temporary measures.

Long-term measures currently on the agenda include upgrading of facilities at Don Muang Airport and achieving a faster passage through customs. The 1998 strategy is to promote Thailand as a safe, high quality destination. Upcountry attractions are being promoted and attempts are being made to curtail environmental damage.

The profile of the typical tourist changes rapidly. In recent years, the fastest rising tourist profile has been the "clean and green" tourist. While rural Thailand can offer the environmentally-sensitive tourist many attractions, one cannot say the same of Bangkok, where air, water and traffic pollution are persistent problems. Figures show that tourists are making shorter stays in the capital, preferring to visit the less polluted provinces. Thailand also wants to attract the higher spending tourist such as the older tourist, who has both money and time to spare.

To attract a better class of tourists, it will be necessary to upgrade existing tourist facilities and add new attractions. Thailand has already made serious attempts to raise the standard of hotel and restaurant service. At last count, there were 80 universities and colleges with training courses in tourism. Competition is fierce for the tourist dollar in Bangkok and service standards are rising. Hotels are constantly engaged in price wars to attract tourists, and some very good packages are provided.

While the government encourages overseas investment in the tourist industry, careful research of the market is essential. Competition will continue to grow as more Thais learn enough English to provide the tourist with the standard of comfort that they demand.

Education

Thais are conscious of globalisation and regard the English language as a means to successfully develop their businesses. Demand for education is still rising and English language teachers can easily find jobs with good salaries. Private universities have sprung up, some of which are joint ventures with overseas universities, while others are Thai investments. Young adults and teenagers are the principal market for education, and schools and colleges are filled to capacity. Universities have annual entrance examinations and quotas in specific fields, such as medicine and veterinary science.

With a good market niche, a precise marketing plan and an active Thai partner, education can be a profitable venture in Thailand, particularly upcountry where the demand for English language skills is growing most rapidly.

The BOI granted international schools, and hotel and business management schools an eight-year tax exemption in 1997. However, to get permission from the Education Board to open a school or college is difficult. You should have a Thai partner to help negotiate such a venture. Choose a partner with good social connections—it will certainly add prestige to your project.

Manufacturing

The government's major role in industry development is to supply the appropriate policy structure to encourage private industry. Other than infrastructure projects, there has been little direct government investment in manufacture, except for financial incentives granted in the way of tax and import duty relief.

Two government agencies that were established to promote manufacture are the BOI in 1960 and the IEAT in 1972. The BOI grants tariff protection, tax holidays and a favourable tax system for imported raw materials and machinery for selected industries.

IEAT encourages manufacture through the planning, development and management of industrial estates and export processing zones throughout the country. There are competing industrial estates in each of the provinces, which aim to draw development away from Bangkok. The largest manufacturing sectors are textiles, motor vehicles and parts, and computer hardware and software.

Textiles

Textile manufacturers have to compete with lower wage countries such as Bangladesh, and are gradually turning to automation to reduce costs. A trained workforce and a market reputation for high quality silk have been established in Thailand, which makes a textile venture, though capital intensive, attractive.

Motor Vehicles and Parts

Thailand aims to position itself as an automotive centre, so the government is highly receptive to the manufacture of vehicles and their parts. This highly-competitive industry is dominated by Japanese and US companies, with Toyota claiming 30% of the local market.

Japanese manufacturers have direct investment, joint venture and technical licensing arrangements in Thailand. Toyota, Isuzu and Mitsubishi control 76% of the local passenger car market and 99% of the commercial vehicle market. US car manufacturers, led by Chrysler, General Motors and Ford, are attempting to enter the market and have experienced some success.

Both Japanese and US manufacturing companies are involved in labour-intensive auto parts production and take advantage of BOI investment incentive schemes that favour exporting industries.

Manufacture of car parts made totally from local materials and designed for export is expected to increase because of the low value of the baht. However, as a result of the financial crisis, local car sales are expected to halve in 1998. All major car manufacturing companies have laid off staff and decreased production runs in direct response to lower local demand.

Computer Equipment and Software

The electronics, computer and telecommunications industries are among the most rapidly developing economic sectors in Thailand. The country aims to position itself as a centre for these industries. To this end, a Microelectronics Research and Development Centre has been set up to create a research base for these industries. The manufacture of computer equipment and software, and the import and distribution of these items are both highly encouraged.

The local market for computer equipment in Thailand has been derived from commercial users such as financial institutions, government agencies and state enterprises, and manufacturing and transportation firms. Demand for computer products is growing at a rate of about 20% a year in the individual sectors.

Japanese firms have a 26% share of the hardware market, edging out US suppliers, who have a 21% share. Dominant US suppliers include IBM, Compaq, DEC and Hewlett-Packard. Most manufacturing investors in Thailand have Japanese origins, and as such, favour Japanese information technology products. The retrofitting of existing equipment and facilities is only now becoming attractive for smaller Thai manufacturers.

Software sales are growing at about 80% a year, though much of the software is pirated. There is also an increasing demand for specialised software like networking and multimedia systems.

Agriculture

The land area under cultivation in Thailand continues to increase as land clearing resumes. By the mid-1990s, land clearing had reached its natural limits. Further increases in rural output will come from improved productivity arising from more efficient practices and from the use of higher-yielding genetic strains.

Rice has traditionally been the main crop of the agricultural sector in Thailand. The bulk of the harvest is reserved for domestic consumption and the surplus is a significant contribution to world rice trade. Rubber is the second most important crop in Thailand and the most important export crop, earning about 50% more export revenue than rice. Thailand is also the world's leading pineapple export country and competes with Australia as the world's top sugar exporter.

Productivity in the rural sector has risen with increased mechanisation. Though employment in the agricultural industry declines each year, output has risen slightly, allowing for the vagaries of the weather. Thai agriculture is steeped in tradition, and Thais hold the view that land is the fundamental asset of the country and cannot be bought over by foreigners.

For investors interested in agriculture, buying and reselling agricultural products is a better option than cultivating them. For example, Thai rice exporters have recently entered negotiations to sell rice to Japan.

Downstream processing, which add value to foodstuffs such as the canning of tropical fruit, also provides opportunities for foreign investors interested in the Thai market. The National Food Institute has been established with the express aim of encouraging

Agricultural Production in Thailand

Commodity	Percentage of Total
Rice	32.1
Rubber	12.6
Sugar	6.9
Cassava	6.0
Maize	4.9
Coconut	1.9
Soy Bean	1.8
Muang Bean	1.2
Oil Palm	1.1
Coffee Bean	0.9

Source: *Pocket Thailand in Figures*

producers to add value to food exports, of which 70% is currently exported in an unprocessed state.

Forestry

Forestry is a much smaller sector by value than agriculture. Old growth forests of traditional timbers, such as mahogany and teak are depleting and other timbers are being cultivated and harvested. Most popular today is wood from the rubber tree, which has a white fine grained finish. It is very popular with the Japanese, who call it white teak.

The Forest Commission is actively trying to conserve the last remaining natural stands of untouched forest through extensive reforestation and education programmes. However, they have not yet managed to halt illegal logging, which threatens even remote areas with the total destruction of natural reserves.

Foreign investment in forestry is restricted to processing raw materials for export.

Fishing is a major industry in the Chon Buri province.

Fishery

Fishing is a significant economic activity in Thailand, which is one of the top 10 marine product producers in the world. Fish products account for about one-quarter the value of agricultural production, which marks seafood products as one of the top 10 export categories by value. Inland freshwater fish farming, river fishing, marine net fishing and oyster farming are the main sources of fishery products.

The overseas market has recently been affected by quality control measures and tariffs imposed by importing countries. The decreased value of the baht could make these products more competitive overseas.

Opportunities exist for the improvement of processing facilities and the development of markets for fishery products.

Construction

Moving around Thailand, one is sometimes struck by the impression that the country has turned into one vast construction site; hence the local joke that the national bird of Thailand is the crane. The amount of construction activity in recent years has been prodigious and too big for the economy to absorb.

Commercial property slumped in the 1990s and residential property grew slowly. Industrial construction was limited to IEAT sites and infrastructure. At the moment, construction activity is devoted mainly to the completion of existing projects.

Residential Property

Of the 6,000 condominiums completed in 1996, only 4,700 were sold, bringing the level of unsold condominiums in Bangkok to about 12,500 units. Rules regarding ownership have been relaxed in an attempt to clear the backlog of empty units. Until recently, foreigners were not allowed to purchase property in Thailand. Now, foreigners can buy physical space, but are still restricted from purchasing the land on which the condominium is built. As Thais dislike buying condominiums, this arrangement is suitable for both property developers and nationalists.

Luxury apartments, largely inhabited by expatriates, are at present about 90% occupied. This figure will be lowered significantly though, as expatriate occupants leave Thailand. About 75%–100% of service apartments are occupied. This figure will also be affected when the expatriates return to their own countries.

Residential property market prices have still not decreased and the Government Housing Bank estimates that 14% of all housing stock in Bangkok is unoccupied. It is safe to assume that residential property is not a good buying or selling proposition.

Industrial Property

The industrial property market is overdeveloped and prices are very competitive. If you want to develop property to sell, you may find a niche in tourism, as outlined above. Buying industrial property, as opposed to building it yourself, seems to be more practical, given the current market. The table below compares the cost of rental with construction costs.

Factory Development Cost, 1996

Location	Construction costs	Rental costs ($ per annum)
Hong Kong	1,260	1,400
Osaka	1,119	269
Shanghai	734	51
Singapore	695	182
Los Angeles	600	50
Kuala Lumpur	377	67
Bangkok	**321**	**96**
Seoul	278	100
Jakarta	200	79

*Figures are in US$ per square metre

Source: KPMG data. Development data is for the cost of a 4,000 sq. m site within 20 km of a major port in a serviced industrial estate. Rental data is for a single floor single span factory with an area of 2,000 sq m

Office space can be rented in an existing building. Rental costs for such property vary widely, depending on location, the quality of the building, the height above street level and the standard of the fit out. The figures in the table below are for "premium" office space, suitable for the headquarters of a substantial business operation.

Rent for Premium Office Space, 1996

Location	US$	Index
Hong Kong	1,236	446
Singapore	1,018	368
Shanghai	741	268
Osaka	699	252
Los Angeles	394	142
Kuala Lumpur	341	123
Seoul	341	123
Bangkok	**277**	**100**
Jakarta	247	89

*Figures are in US$ per square metre

Source: KPMG data

The 1996 figures quoted would have declined considerably, forced down, in US$ terms, not only by the property slump but also by the decline in the value of the baht and the currency of other Southeast Asian countries. According to a worldwide study on rental levels issued in 1997 by Richard Ekkis, Bangkok office rental is now the cheapest in Asia.

Commercial Property

Hotels   There has been an oversupply of hotels in the last four years. There are about 250,000 hotel rooms in Thailand, with about 65,000 in Bangkok alone. Occupancy rate is between 50% and 60%. Hotels are either a very good investment if you think the tourist industry will meet the goals set for it by the TAT or a very bad one if tourists stay away from Thailand.

Malls   In the early 1990s, developers invested heavily in malls. Today, however, many shop spaces in these malls are empty and some have closed. Others are looking for lower-end tenants, which did not feature in the initial plans. Anchor tenants get very good rent rates.

With careful research—particularly for accessibility to the mall—such enterprises might succeed and those that are well-developed will be in a good position when the economy recovers. At present, it is best that foreign investors in malls form joint ventures with Thai partners.

Infrastructure Projects

Opportunities exist for foreign investors interested in infrastructure development projects. These include power generation and transmission, petroleum refining and petrochemicals, telecommunications, transportation, environment, healthcare, and defence equipment sectors. One of the best ways to get into these areas is through government bids.

Selling to the Government

The key to successful bidding on Thai government contracts and supply tenders is to have a reputable local representative with easy access to the procuring agency and good knowledge of the specific requirements and practices. Without the assistance of an effective representative, it is very difficult to sell to the government.

Foreign Bids
The "Prime Minister's Procurement Regulations" govern public sector procurement. Under these regulations, local bidders are favoured, at least theoretically. In the evaluation of bids by the government, foreign bids incur an immediate 15% cost penalty over local bids.

Mall development projects are normally huge, expensive and well-planned. However, these factors do not necessarily guarantee crowds.

Local representatives are an accepted and legitimate part of the bidding process. Agents often alert overseas firms to attractive tenders, sometimes even before the tenders are issued. They will work to ensure that the products of their principal are chosen.

Energy

The Electricity Generating Authority of Thailand (EGAT), the Thai state enterprise involved in electric power generation, is the principal customer in Thailand. However, recently, there have been moves to allow increased private sector participation in electric power generation in Thailand. This will also offer opportunities for other electrical service providers and distributors.

Oil

Thailand is a net oil importer. In 1991, the country eliminated domestic oil price controls and took measures to liberalise the market. As a result of these efforts, the market share of small companies in Thailand's retail oil product distribution sector is expected to increase significantly by the year 2000. By that time, Thailand may have as many as 13,000 petrol stations, with the market share for small companies reaching 30–35%.

In June 1977, the National Energy Policy Committee (NEPC) resolved to remove all barriers to the establishment and expansion of oil refineries in Thailand. This means that all existing companies can set up new refineries or increase their production without first getting government permission. Entrepreneurs will no longer have to pay levies of 2% of revenue to the government but will be subject only to the guidelines and taxes of other industries.

Natural Gas

There are substantial fields of natural gas in the Gulf of Thailand. These finds have prompted the development of the Petrochemical Complex on the eastern seaboard. Additional fields are being developed in the Andaman Sea off south-west Thailand and near the Burmese border. Unocal Thailand is the largest gas producer in the country.

About 85% of Thailand's gas consumption is used for electricity generation and the remainder is used for industrial purposes. Gas demand was expected to grow along with the economy, turning Thailand into a large potential market for imported liquefied natural gas (LNG). However, if the new fields come on line as expected and the economy grows as modestly as it seems likely to do, Thailand will be largely self-sufficient in natural gas by 2005.

Transportation

Air   Thailand is located in the centre of Asia's air traffic. With a projected annual traffic growth of 9%, its main airport, Bangkok's Don Muang, will reach its capacity of 16 million passengers by the year 2000. As 81% of tourists to Thailand arrive by air through Don Muang, a major increase in airport capacity will be required.

To relieve the pressure on airport terminal facilities, the Thai Government is considering building a second international airport at Nong Ngu Hao, about 18 miles (47 km) east of Bangkok, at a cost of about $4 billion. Construction contracts will present opportunities for a large number of bidders in the construction industry. This project's visibility waxes and wanes with changes in government but it is necessary, in light of Thailand's increased dependence on the tourist industry.

Land   The need for efficient, high quality road construction continues. Demand for new roads and the need to complete existing projects provide opportunities for high capital, long-term investors. These opportunities exist in overhead road and rail construction in Bangkok, as well as in highway construction in outlying regions.

Communications

There are 1.2 million reminders—the number of applicants on Bangkok's waiting list for telephone lines—that Thailand has significant telecommunications needs. Opportunities to supply telephone switching equipment, optic fibre cables, mobile telephones, paging systems, private automatic branch exchanges, facsimile machines, cable TV broadcasting network equipment and satellite signal receiving equipment are plentiful. In 1993, Thailand imported $571 million worth of telecommunications equipment, up 94% since 1989.

After more than a century of monopoly-based telecommunications services, the Thai Ministry of Transportation and Communication (MOTC) is opening its doors to the private sector. Opportunities exist in a number of areas.

Quality and reliability are the most important factors in clinching sales in Thailand's telecommunications market. In addition, costs and financing are often vital to closing a deal. Local telecommunications service providers usually receive concessionary loans as well as suppliers' long-term credits. Companies can enhance their credentials as bidders with the help of prudent and experienced Thai partners.

Other Infrastructure Developments

Among other infrastructure projects on the drawing boards are two port development projects: the Eastern Seaboard Development Project at Rayong and the Southern Seaboard Development Project between Krabi province and Khanom in the Surat Thani Province in southern Thailand. The latter project includes two deep sea ports, a natural gas separation plant, two petrochemical complexes, 2,800 acres of industrial estates and an airport. Most of these projects will provide opportunities for sub-contracting.

Mining and Minerals

In all, Thailand produces more than 40 different kinds of minerals, although development is uneven. New minerals are discovered regularly and include iron ore, lignite, dolomite and laolinite, antimony, barite, copper, feldspar, fluorite, gypsum, lead ore, potash and zinc. The value of all of these minerals is subject to price fluctuations in the commodity markets.

After Brazil, Indonesia and Malaysia, Thailand is the world's fourth largest producer of tin, its most important metal. The second most important is zinc. Almost the entire output of tin and zinc is exported from Thailand.

Other minerals found in Thailand are gemstones, in particular rubies and sapphires, which have been in the top 10 list of both import and export value in recent years. Although many of the older gem mines have depleted, Thailand hopes to become the Asian centre for gem cutting.

Any investment in minerals should concentrate on processing local minerals for export or on importing equipment for extraction and processing.

Environmental Technology

Thailand's years of market driven economic growth have taken its toll on the environment. For many years, the government has paid lip service to addressing Thailand's environmental problems. This may translate into action as problems exacerbate. Providing remedies to such problems as air and water pollution is likely to offer future opportunities for enterprises specialising in environmental technology.

Thailand has restructured its environmental agency, now called the Ministry of Science, Technology and Environment (MOSTE) and has established an environmental fund with a projected annual budget of $80 million. Like other ASEAN countries, the Thai Government is focusing on the total elimination of leaded gasoline by the year 1998. Other issues include limiting the dumping of hazardous wastes and encouraging the efficient use of energy.

State planners will install a 15 megawatt solar power generating facility in Thailand during the Eighth National Plan running from 1997 to 2001. Thailand is the first country in Southeast Asia with a government-sponsored programme to use solar power.

One specific business opportunity exists in solid waste handling, where 3,000 two-tonne garbage trucks are needed to remove the daily waste produced by Bangkok residents. By the year 2000, Bangkok may require as many as 5,500 garbage trucks. As the Thai Government focuses on cleaning up its environmental act, the market for such products may increase further.

Overall, the market for environmental products in Thailand is growing at 20–25% a year. The market is estimated to yield returns of between US$4.8 billion and US$9.5 billion over the next decade.

Healthcare Technology

Thailand is the largest market for healthcare services in Southeast Asia. In 1991, Thailand spent $3.5 billion on healthcare—almost 6% of its GDP—a figure greater than the total health expenditures of Singapore, Malaysia and the Philippines.

Thai imports of medical equipment, valued at $64 million in 1989, will grow at an estimated 44% over the next five years. Because the industry's needs are so great and the government does not have the resources to meet this demand, private investors are beginning to set up private hospitals in Thailand. In 1997, there were 127 government hospitals and 70 private hospitals operating in Thailand, as well as 2,800 clinics.

Emerging Sectors

The assessment of business opportunities presented by the various sectors of the economy is carried out by various commercial and government institutions. Siam Bank's evaluation of growth areas in the Thai economy is outlined below.

Growth Areas of the Thai Economy

Service Industry
Travel and tourism services

Consumer Products and Services
Soft drinks, alcohol, restaurants, entertainment and services, cosmetics and toiletries

Industrial Products
Telecommunications and telecommunications equipment; computer software; aircraft and aircraft parts; electrical power systems; computers and peripherals; food processing and packaging equipment; industrial chemicals; process controls; industrial defence; industry equipment; medical equipment; plastic material and resins; construction equipment; building products; pumps, valves, and compressors; laboratory and scientific instruments; machine tools and metalworking equipment; pollution control equipment; and plastics production machinery

Infrastructure
- Energy: architectural, construction, oil and gas field machinery
- Environmental technology

Health
Dental equipment

Stable areas of the Thai economy include:
- Agriculture, livestock, and transport and medical service

Areas of the Thai economy that are slowing down include:
- Property and related building material, hotels and tourism, and retailing
- Exported food products

Summary

With the benefit of hindsight, there is no doubt that Thailand lived beyond its means in the early 1990s. The growth rate was too high. Consumption was too conspicuous. Anti-corruption legislation was ineffective. Political leaders allowed conflicts of interest to develop between their business interests and their public duties. Banks lent too much on too little security. Property development was embraced too enthusiastically and the quality of properties was too poor.

In short, Thailand had a boom. Like most countries, the first years of emergence from the boom will require economic adjustment. Paradoxically, such periods are often the periods of greatest opportunity for business. Asset prices are down. Costs are low. Labour is readily available. Incentive schemes are enhanced. The barriers to foreign investment are decreasing. In fact, people with opposing economic philosophies would argue that the investment climate has never been better.

From the mid-1990s until the beginning of the next century, forecasts of Thailand's likely growth rate have become lower.

Stronger emphasis on sustainable development and science and technology are evident as Thailand joins the ranks of Newly Industrialised Economies (NICs). As of 1994, Thailand has a domestic market of around 60 million people, with rapidly increasing purchasing power (per capita income is US$2,500 and it is projected to reach US$3,860 by the year 2000).

Continuing liberalisation of the tax and tariff structures, an open-door policy towards foreign investment and macroeconomic stability will keep Thailand a favoured investment location. Increasing political stability and a trend towards regional cooperation within ASEAN and the countries of the Greater Mekong Sub-region will attract more worldwide attention to the region as a whole.

Thailand's role in this new regional order will be crucial as its entrepreneurial leadership develops and its strengths evolve beyond being merely a cost-effective labour platform to greater industrial capability, diversity and depth.

Thailand is well-positioned to serve as a regional base for investment in the emerging economies of the region. The government is actively forging links with the countries of the Greater Mekong. The country's newly-established offshore banking facility—the Bangkok International Banking Facilities (BIBF)—will further enhance trade and investment between Thailand and its regional neighbours.

With the successful completion of the Uruguay Round of GATT negotiations, the country is on course to continue as an export powerhouse. Its rapidly growing domestic market is also attracting foreign investors.

Diversification offers investors a stable investment environment because Thailand does not depend upon one product or type of industry for its economic stability. Among the many expanding opportunities in investment, there is the agriculture and agro industry, the manufacturing sector, and the service sector. Thailand is already one of the major food exporters in the world.

There are other areas of economic growth. Thailand is still emerging as a major exporter. Opportunities exist in fundamental manufacturing, assembly, components manufacture, assembly industries and other support industry.

Thailand is a major tourist destination and the service industry goes along with that. This includes consumer industries, technology support, research and development activities, tourism related industries, and business and financial advising services.

As Thailand begins its ascent up the value-added ladder, it is starting to produce domestically, a greater share of the capital goods, parts, and components that fuel the manufacturing engine. Tremendous investment opportunities are implicit in this process.

CHAPTER 5

Establishing a Business

As a nation, Thailand wants your business. Thailand also wants to retain its own economic sovereignty, as it always has. These are of course opposing objectives.

Historically, Thailand's method of resolving this conflict has been to allow foreign business to operate within the country under a string of conditions that enable Thais to retain control of their own destinies. At the same time, they offer foreign businesses access to local labour and some local trade.

In recent years, the balance between imposing conditions on foreign business and offering investment incentives has tilted in favour of incentives. Thailand's deteriorating external account has forced the country to relax the conditions of foreign business entry and offer increasing business concessions. Thailand needs foreign investment merely to balance its external account.

Nonetheless, bureaucratic interference is deeply-seated. At the operating level, you may feel that the laws of the country are framed to frustrate your business. Thailand can certainly tie up your company's administrators in red tape. You may even start to believe that the passive resistance of the bureaucracy is giving you the message that foreign business is not wanted.

This is not the case. Thailand is equally capable of tying its own businesses up with bureaucratic red tape. At the petty bureaucratic level, Thais have yet to learn that their function in life is not to impede but to assist their customers—a problem in many developing countries. At present, the bureaucracy expects you to be persistent.

Perhaps more serious barriers than bureaucratic resistance are the complicated specifications regulating foreign ownership and control of companies. There are also several sectors in which foreigners are simply prohibited from participation.

Business Categories

There are three distinctive categories of businesses in Thailand. Category A is closed to aliens (the legal term for foreigners in Thailand). Category B businesses are also prohibited to aliens unless approval is granted by the Board of Investment (BOI). Category C businesses are open to foreigners but under a range of restrictions that depend on a number of factors such as the nature of the business, the location of the business within Thailand, the presence or absence of Thai partners, and the nationality of the foreign applicant. These rules will be more fully detailed later in this chapter.

To do business in category C, you must apply to the Department of Commercial Registration.

The three categories are not mutually exclusive. The only way to determine the status of your business is to apply for a licence. Approval of a licence application depends not only on the nature of your business but also on how you phrase your intentions on your licence application. Ask your adviser for help.

The different business included in the three categories, as stated by the Board of Investment, are outlined below.

Category A (Closed)

- Traditional agriculture such as rice growing
- Commercial business such as internal trade in local agricultural products and land trade
- Some service businesses such as accounting, law, architecture, advertising, brokerage and construction

Category B (Closed Unless Approved)

- Agricultural pursuits such as cultivation, orchard farming, animal husbandry, timber, fishing, industrial and handicraft businesses
- Commercial businesses such as retailing, ore trading, selling of food and drinks, and trade of antiques
- Service industries such as tour agencies, hotels, photography, laundering, dressmaking, and other businesses such as land, water and air transportation

Category C (Open)

- Commercial businesses, such as wholesale trade, except items included in category A
- All exporting, retailing of machinery, equipment and tools, selling of food and beverages to promote tourism
- A select list of industrial and handicraft businesses, which includes manufacture of animal feed, vegetable oil refining, textile manufacture, manufacture of glass ware, manufacture of food bowls and plates, manufacture of stationery and printing paper, mining, including rock salt mining, service businesses, and other businesses not listed in A or B

Regulatory Authorities

While the Board of Investment (BOI) is the principal body regulating foreign investment in Thailand, you will not satisfy the bureaucratic process merely with a visit to the BOI. Thailand is a country of competing bureaucracies. Other government agencies need to be involved as well (as indicated in chapter 2).

Generally, aliens in Thailand have the same legal rights as Thai citizens but have restricted rights to investing and working in the country.

If your corporation is an alien as defined by the Alien Business Law, your business activities may be restricted. In general,

The Alien Business Law

The most important statute for foreign investors in Thailand is the Alien Business Law, which states that an alien is a natural person or a juristic person (from now on called a corporation) without Thai nationality including:

- A corporation with half or more than half of the capital belonging to aliens
- A corporation where half or more than half of the number of its shareholders, partners or members are aliens
- A limited partnership or a registered ordinary partnership which has an alien manager

permission will be granted if the Thais are satisfied that your business will be beneficial to the economy. This criterion includes most legitimate business activities.

Firms engaging in production activities must also register with the Ministry of Industry and the Ministry of Labour.

In addition, you may or may not need an Alien Business Licence depending on the nature of the business. To determine your specific position, it will be necessary to consult a Thai lawyer specialising in this area. Apart from that, in the initial stages of a project, most of your dealings will be with the BOI.

Government Guarantees

In consideration of the investor's decision to invest, the government offers some security guarantees to safeguard the investor's investment. The government guarantees that it will not:

- Establish competing businesses in the industry
- Grant tax relief to competing imported goods
- Impose price controls on the company's products
- Nationalise the investment
- Withhold permission to export

These guarantees will be honoured as long as Thailand wants to encourage foreign investment.

The Board of Investment (BOI)

The BOI's role is to maintain a strategic alliance with industry to achieve national economic objectives. The BOI maintains and continually upgrades a list of economic activities considered to be in the national interest and offers development incentives to both local and foreign private firms in these areas.

BOI Incentives

Projects eligible for BOI incentives include industries that:

- Significantly strengthen Thailand's balance of payments position, especially through production for export
- Support the development of the country's resources
- Substantially increase employment
- Locate operations in provinces outside the Bangkok metropolitan area
- Conserve energy or replace imported energy supplies
- Establish or develop industries that form the base for further technological development
- Are considered important and necessary by the government
- Supply transport systems
- Build public utilities and basic infrastructure
- Offer protection and/or restoration of the environment

Source: Board of Investment (1996)

Projects approved by the BOI attract investment incentives such as favourable land deals, import tariff relief and tax breaks on corporate earnings, which are available to both domestic and foreign-owned enterprises.

In 1993, the BOI initiated a major shift in emphasis from export orientation to industrial decentralisation as its major policy goal. This policy is intended to increase development outside the Bangkok metropolitan area to the countryside where the population is employed primarily in the labour-intensive agricultural sector (which accounted for only 12% of Thailand's GDP in 1993).

A 1997 investment incentive package granted duty exemptions on electronics manufacturers, developers of mass transit projects, commercial airports, maritime transport companies, producers of electric or steam power, research and development institutions, and aircraft parts manufacturers.

Generally, the economic activities rated as being the most important are those that bring new technology to Thailand. Firms proposing such developments are likely to attract the most generous investment incentives, as are those that relocate industry in less congested and polluted areas, provide employment for Thais in rural areas and raise the standard of the Thai workforce.

The BOI's list of strategic activities is continually reassessed as the country's economic landscape changes or as new industries emerge and mature industries become obsolete. Consult the annual BOI list for further information.

Applying for BOI Assistance

Applications must be submitted in the correct format and applicants should be meticulous about providing all the details requested by the BOI, including all the supporting documentation requested. Applications can be filed in the name of a natural person or in the name of a corporation.

The BOI usually decides within 60 days whether or not a project is eligible for investment privileges. Prospective investors should note that there is often competition by other firms for a BOI incentive package. To protect the interests of the successful applicant and to maximise the chances of the project's success, unsuccessful applicants are prohibited from further investment in Thailand in industries similar to the approved project.

After the BOI approves an application, it will issue a Notification of Approval within 15 days. The Notification of Approval will state the privileges and conditions, and inform the applicant of the specific procedures that will be required to officially receive final approval of the project. Upon receipt of the letter of Notification of Approval, the approved applicant should furnish the BOI with written acceptance within one month.

Under BOI rules, once an application is granted, other applicants are excluded from investment assistance. This puts responsibility on the BOI to ensure that the investor is not dilatory about proceeding with his investment. Therefore, the developer must meet various dates for the submission of documentation and the completion of the project.

Documents to be Submitted to BOI
Within six months of acceptance by the developer, the following documents must be furnished to the BOI:

- Memorandum of Association
- Certificate of Business Registration
- Certificate stating registered capital, list of authorised directors and address of the head office
- List of shareholders
- A document evidencing remittance of foreign currency issued by the Bank of Thailand for foreign investors
- Joint Venture Contract
- Application form to obtain the BOI's Promotion Certificate

Assuming these documents are satisfactory, the developer will be issued a Promotion Certificate entitling him to proceed with the project. Once the Promotion Certificate has been issued, the investor must start construction within six months of the acceptance date stated on the certificate.

Award conditions additionally require that all machinery and equipment exempted from import duties be delivered within 24 months of the acceptance date. Construction of the facility must also be completed within 30 months of the acceptance date.

The BOI's safeguards might seem onerous to some investors but when approval has been granted, they are beneficial to your business as they remove all other competition.

BOI Application Approvals

The number of applications made to the BOI doubled between 1991 and 1995 while the approval rate varied between 96% in 1991 and 85% in 1995. However, the number of approved projects that started operations has dropped sharply. The table below indicates the history of BOI applications, approvals and businesses started between 1991 and 1995.

BOI Investment Programme			
	Applications Made	Applications Approved	Projects Started
1991	631	605 (96%)	434 (71%)
1992	444	381 (85%)	338 (88%)
1993	1255	869 (69%)	377 (43%)
1994	1538	1191 (77%)	314 (26%)
1995	1407	1197 (85%)	323 (26%)

A country's overall economy is affected by economic cycles and Thailand's economy is currently suffering a downturn. Some sectors continue to grow even in a downturn. If your business is immune to the external environment or can capitalise on it (and only you and your advisers can determine how your business will be affected), then go ahead with your application to the BOI and invest in Thailand.

BOI Approved Projects

The largest number of investors applying for privileges were Thai companies—accounting for 67.7% of the applications for BOI incentives. Many of the nominally Thai projects were joint ventures with foreign partners, under arrangements where Thai companies provided most of the funds and foreign firms the technology.

Projects with foreign participation tend to be larger. In 1995, joint venture projects with foreign partners accounted for 50% of all investments and 60% of all investment costs. The largest sums of money went to services and infrastructure projects, followed by chemicals, paper and plastics.

Foreign countries which applied on their own behalf for promotional privileges in 1995 were Japan with 13.9% of the number of applications, followed by the United States with 4.9%, Taiwan with 3 %, Australia with 1.7% and the rest of the world with 8.8%.

Ownership Laws

Several restrictions apply to the ownership of companies and their activities. Only companies that comply with these ownership guidelines are eligible for BOI investment incentives. The following table summarises the rules as they were in 1997.

BOI Ownership Guidelines

Production Exported (% of)	Minimum Thai Ownership
<50%	51%
>50 - 100%	"less than 50%"
100%	0%

Note that regardless of the given figures, for "Resource Projects" such as agriculture, animal husbandry, fisheries, mineral exploration and mining, Thai nationals must hold at least 60% of the registered capital.

Decentralisation

Thailand has an active policy of promoting development in its rural areas. In particular, the government wishes to see investment directed away from specific locations, such as Bangkok, which are considered to be overdeveloped. To implement this objective, the government offers additional financial incentives to encourage investment in regional areas. The choice of location may, therefore, boil down to a choice between an established area with good facilities and a new area with good incentives.

The Thai Government has adopted three overlapping methods of dividing the country into economic areas. The areas in the divisions are as follows:

- Areas within the country are designated as one of three "zones", roughly based on their distance from Bangkok.
- Within each zone, there are likely to be "industrial estates", where new industries are encouraged to locate—based on the government's social objective of segregating domestic and industrial land use.
- A "free trade zone" or an "Export Processing Zone (EPZ)" may exist near an industrial estate in which the government may encourage new industries to locate.

Zones and Industrial Estates

Several areas have been allocated to the three zones. Of the 76 provinces of Thailand, 63 are in zone 2 or zone 3.

In addition, 44 industrial estates have been set up in 18 provinces. Of these, 18 are private estates, 19 are joint ventures between the government and the private sector, and eight are entirely government projects.

The seven most highly developed estates are in Rayong, on the southern coast of Thailand. These offer good infrastructure, a deep water port and a skilled workforce. The other popular areas are Chon Buri, Sara Buri, Bangkok and Samut Prakan, each with four estates.

Zone 1   It includes Bangkok, Samut Prakan, Samut Sakhon, Pathum Thani, Nonta Buri and Nakhon Pathom.

Incentives for Zone 1

The following investment incentives are available for approved projects establishing in Zone 1:

Incentive	Import duty reduction on machinery subject to tariff reduction by the Ministry of Finance
Concession	50% on duty greater than 10% of the landed value of the equipment
Conditions	80% of sales must be exported or the factory must be located in an approved industrial estate
Incentive	Reduction of corporate income tax
Concession	Three-year exemption from tax
Conditions	80% of sales must be exported and the factory must be located in approved industrial estates or approved free trade zones
Incentive	Import duty reduction on raw materials
Concession	Full duty for one year
Conditions	30% of sales must be exported

Zone 2 It includes Samut Songkhram, Ratchaburi, Kanchanaburi, Suphanburi, Angthong, Ayutthaya, Saraburi, Nakhon Nayok, Chachoengsao and Chon Buri.

Incentives for zone 2 are the same as zone 1 except that additional incentives are available for the import of machinery. (For zone 1, this import concession is limited to machinery subject to tariff reduction by the Ministry of Finance.)

Incentives for Zone 2

Incentive	Import duty reduction on all machinery
Concession	50% on duty greater than 10%
Conditions	80% of sales must be exported or the factory must be located in approved industrial estates

Incentive	Reduction of corporate income tax
Concession	Three-year exemption from tax
Conditions	80% of sales must be exported and the factory must be located in approved industrial estates or approved free trade zones

Incentive	Import duty reduction on raw materials
Concession	Full duty for one year
Conditions	30% of sales must be exported

Zone 3 It includes the rest of Thailand. Additional incentives apply across the board for projects in Zone 3 areas.

Incentives for Zone 3

Incentive	Import duty reduction on all machinery
Concession	Total exemption
Conditions	80% of sales must be exported or the factory must be located in approved industrial estates

Incentive	Reduction of corporate income tax
Concession	Eight-year exemption from tax plus 50% reduction of tax for the ensuing five years after the eight-year period
Conditions	80% of sales must be exported and the factory must be located in approved industrial estates or approved free trade zones

Incentive	Import duty reduction on raw materials for exported products
Concession	Full duty for one year
Conditions	30% of sales must be exported

Incentive	Import duty reduction on raw materials for domestic products
Concession	75% of duty for five years
Conditions	Provided materials of comparable quality are not being produced in Thailand

Incentive	Double reduction for cost of utilities
Concession	Double reduction of utility costs from taxable income for 10 years
Conditions	None

Export Processing Zones (EPZ)

In addition to partitioning the country into three economic zones, Thailand has several Export Processing Zones (EPZ). Firms located in EPZs are exempt from import duties and other taxes on factory construction materials, machinery and equipment, and export manufacturing inputs. Within EPZs, foreign investors are permitted to own land and employ foreign technicians and experts.

In addition, within EPZs, the Customs Department allows larger firms engaged exclusively in manufacturing for export to set up bonded warehouses and to import (duty-free) inputs for their export production. Producers who receive approval to establish bonded warehouses must pay an annual fee and submit guarantees for duties.

Other Investment Incentives
For a long time, Thailand has not permitted aliens to own land and buildings. However, this is one of the restrictions that is presently being relaxed, in view of the 1997 collapse of the property market and the large number of unsold speculative building projects on the books.

In the second half of 1997, property prices in Thailand were well below building costs, representing a buying opportunity that has been unrivalled in the past 10 years.

Tax Treaties
Thailand has double tax treaties with several countries. Among other benefits available under these treaties, foreign institutional investors can enjoy the privilege of tax-free capital gains.

Countries with which Thailand has tax treaties are: Australia, Austria, Belgium, Canada, China, Denmark, Finland, France, Germany, Hungary, India, Indonesia, Italy, Japan, Korea. Malaysia, the Netherlands, Norway, Pakistan, Philippines, Poland, Singapore, Sri Lanka, Sweden, United Kingdom and Vietnam.

On the other hand, the United States is one country with which Thailand does not have a reciprocal tax treaty. Americans working in Thailand are still double-taxed, which to some extent dampens US involvement in Thailand. Americans contemplating working in Thailand can check their rights and entitlements with a taxation agent.

Special Relations with the United States

Under the Treaty of Amity and Economic Relations between the United States and Thailand in 1966, the Thai Government grants the United States special privileges under which the United States is excused from most of the rules relating to foreign investors from other countries. The treaty exempts US businesses operating in Thailand from most foreign exchange restrictions imposed by the Alien Business Decree. US citizens and businesses incorporated in the United States or Thailand, in which US citizens have majority share, are allowed to engage in business on the same basis as Thais. This is perhaps why the United States, unlike other nations, finds doing business in Thailand easier.

Consequently, a US corporation may set up a wholly-owned subsidiary company or branch office in Thailand, with restrictions only in the fields of communications, transport and banking, as well as fields where there is exploitation of land or natural resources, and domestic trade in indigenous agricultural products. To register under the treaty, a US company has to file an application with the Department of Commercial Registration at the Ministry of Commerce. In return, Thais are extended reciprocal rights to invest in the United States.

Relations between the United States and Thailand are good, although trade issues—in particular protection of intellectual property rights—dominate the bilateral agenda. The US & Foreign Commercial Service office at the American Embassy provides valuable assistance in locating potential representatives and partners, and in obtaining preliminary market information. The Foreign Agricultural Service office at the American Embassy also supplies lists of agricultural product importers.

At the recent Uruguay Round of GATT negotiations, Thailand agreed to liberalise its investment regime within 10 years and grant to all foreigners the same privileges granted to American investors.

Registering a US Company

American companies have a number of privileges in Thailand not available to people of other nationalities. One is that they can set up a branch office of their own business in Thailand.

As outlined in a 1994 CIA report, to set up a branch office in Thailand, the documents to be submitted are as follows:

- A Certificate of Incorporation (The Memorandum of Association, the Articles of Association and the Certificate of Incorporation should all show foreign incorporation).
- Power of Attorney appointing a person to be in charge of the operation in Thailand, together with a Thai translation. A work permit for a foreign manager must also be submitted to the Department of Commercial Registration.
- A letter describing details of the project (business activities of the overseas company, purpose of establishing representative in Thailand, plan for a period of five years of the representative office, place of business in Thailand, activities to be performed by the representative office, benefits of establishment of the representative office and appointment of a manager).
- A lease agreement of the business premises.

The first two items must be certified by a competent officer of the country of the head office and endorsed by a notary public at the Thai embassy or consulate.

The representative office is permitted to operate for a period of five years, during which the company must comply with the conditions pursuant to the Ministerial Regulations in accordance with NEC 281 which states that:

- The maximum amount of the loan used for the operations for the approved activities must not exceed seven times the owner's equity
- There must be a remittance of not less than 5,000,000 baht in foreign currency to be used for the approved activities in Thailand

- At least one person responsible for the operation in Thailand must have a domicile in the country

Business enterprises from countries other than the United States must incorporate a Thai commercial operation before they can begin trading. This is not necessarily a daunting task, but requires the approval of the Department of Commercial Registration at the Ministry of Commerce.

Business Structure in Thailand

Several options exist for structuring a business organisation in Thailand. Company structures in Thailand are similar to Western concepts. The options on business arrangements are as follows:

- A sole proprietorship
- Partnership
- Registered partnership
- Unregistered partnership
- Limited partnership
- Limited company
- Closely-held company
- Publicly-held company
- Branch of a foreign-owned business

Limited liability companies may be either privately-owned or publicly-listed. The majority of companies operating in Thailand are privately-owned limited liability companies. Most foreign companies in Thailand operate as private limited companies, which are allowed to offer shares to the public.

In general, the law pertaining to individual industries limits foreign ownership of companies listed on the Stock Exchange of Thailand to a maximum of 15%. There are however, exceptions. In a few cases, majority foreign ownership of listed companies is allowed by law.

Need for a Local Attorney

Executing distributorship agreements and setting up offices in Thailand are not complex tasks but do require the services of lawyers. Lawyers finalise a company's standard distributorship agreement and register firms, help to obtain the requisite permits and advise on the various types of business organisations. Lawyers are also needed to register patents and trademarks, as well as to protect your product from intellectual property rights infringement through the appropriate legal procedures.

Lawyers in Thailand are in oversupply, so finding one to act for you is not difficult. Some lawyers advertise one stop shopping—with a whole range of legal services, from visa applications to company registrations, and any other requirements you may have. Contact several law firms to find one that best suits your needs and budget, and try to get a lawyer with a good knowledge of English so as to avoid unnecessary complications.

Joint Ventures

The most common way of entering a new market in Thailand is by joint venture. In some cases, depending on the product and its market, joint venturing may be the only corporate arrangement permitted. Local production through a joint venture may be the most convenient way to get your product onto the Thai market, particularly if import duty is high on the item being manufactured.

Finding a joint venture partner in the Thai community is not difficult. Thai firms are gradually moving up the technological ladder to overcome rising labour costs and compete for regional markets in Southeast Asia, Indo-China, and southern China. Many Thai firms actively seek joint venture partners that can bring technical, technological, marketing and management skills into their businesses. In turn, the Thai firms usually provide capital and offer contacts with the local business community. The Thai joint venture can also serve as a base for entry into the entire Southeast Asian market.

Import-export Businesses

The simplest business arrangement with Thailand involves exporting goods or services to the country (Thai imports) and importing goods from the country (Thai exports). Furthermore, if these dealings are conducted through a Thai agent, you might not even have to start a business establishment in Thailand. Alternatively, you could establish an agent's office in Thailand.

Agreements between suppliers and agents/distributors are governed by the general contract law under the Thailand Civil and Commercial Code. The relationship between the two parties is basically a buyer-seller relationship under a sale of goods contract. Under such an arrangement, responsibility will be borne by the import agent. Entering into a formal agent/distributor arrangement also prevents any Value Added Tax (VAT) exposure under the Thai Revenue Code.

Import Controls

The Ministry of Commerce has designated certain classes of goods as being subject to import controls. The purpose of this is to protect locally made goods against foreign competition. The act which controls imports is the Controlling Importation and Exportation of Goods Act (1979)—45 different categories of goods are restricted under the act. Details of restricted goods can also be obtained from the Ministry of Commerce.

To obtain approval to import goods on the restricted list, licences must be obtained from the Ministry of Commerce. A Thai hotel building contractor, when asked what the most difficult part of his job was, answered that it was importing building materials. His solution was simple—pay someone else to take the punishment, that is, illegal building materials. However, this is not a recommended procedure for a foreign importer.

Goods on the restricted list include drugs, chemicals, certain raw materials, petroleum, industrial products, textiles, agricultural products and a range of food products, including powdered skim milk and fresh milk, potatoes, soy beans and soy bean oil, refined sugar, and corn for animal feed, among others.

Many licensing requirements will be eliminated as Thailand completes the adjustments necessary to conform to its Uruguay Round commitments. Particular licensing regulations apply to food and pharmaceutical product importers who are required to apply for import licences from the Thai Food and Drug Administration.

A Costly Process

The licensing process is time-consuming and costly, and requires the disclosure of proprietary information. Licences cost US$600 per item. Products imported in bulk require laboratory analysis at a cost of $40 to $120 per item. Products imported in sealed containers (consumer-ready packaged) require laboratory analysis at a cost of $200 per item. Some 39 items must be registered as "specific controlled food items" at an additional cost of $200. Although the Thai Food and Drug Administration has made efforts to streamline the registration process, it usually requires three months or more to complete the application.

Note: Prices are approximated, given the fluctuations in the value of the baht.

Import Quotas

Quotas, like tariffs, are designed to protect local suppliers. Once a quota becomes established in the bureaucracy, a change in the local supply situation may not help get the quota relaxed, even if all local suppliers were to go out of business.

The Skimmed Milk Shortage
During the first part of 1997, skimmed milk was a commodity subject to quotas. As a result, dairy operators were forced to close their factories one by one as requests for much needed skim milk powder imports went unheeded by the Agriculture and Agricultural Cooperatives Ministry.

In actual fact, the imports had arrived. However, because authorities had not officially approved the quota, the Agricultural and Agriculture Cooperatives Ministry did not allow Nestle and other dairy operators to collect their goods.

Prohibited Imports

Few imported products are prohibited, aside from drugs and firearms. Other forbidden imports include aerosol mixtures of vinyl chloride monomers and products with trademark infringements.

A large number of products also require import licences. Details can be obtained from the Customs Department.

Tariffs and Duties

Thailand maintains significant tariff barriers, with current duty rates at 10% to 15% for a majority of the products on which duties are collected. However, duty exemptions are routinely granted to firms with investment promotion privileges. Rebates of import duties on raw materials are granted upon the export of the finished products. This rebate, like the VAT rebate, is often very slow in being refunded.

Along with most other countries, at the 1993 GATT Uruguay Round, Thailand committed itself to reducing import duties. In compliance with this commitment, a simplified import regime will, in future, result in a system of only 5 or 6 rates and a maximum duty of 30% for almost all products.

High tariffs remain major barriers to value-added agricultural products and apparel. Tariffs are high for most agricultural products

Tariff Reduction
In 1997, a tariff reduction regime had been under way for some years. Duties on most types of machinery were reduced from 30–40% to just 5% in 1990. Similar duty reductions were made on imported computers and parts in 1991. Duties were lowered on ferrous metals and chemicals in January 1993 and nonferrous metals and many miscellaneous items in January 1994. In March 1994, reductions were announced on 417 items (mechanical, electrical, and optical/measuring/medical categories). The average duties on the items fell from 28% to 14%, and in some cases duties were almost totally eliminated (e.g. medical equipment).

such as beef, turkey, fresh and dried fruits and nuts, fruit juice, and soybean meal. Duties on wine and spirits are 60% of the value or a specific duty ranging from 10 to 110 baht per litre (depending on the variety), whichever is higher. Imported alcoholic beverages have separate excise duties varying from 10% to 48%.

Separate excise duties are assessed on a number of other imported products such as tobacco, and some electrical and petroleum products. Many textile and apparel products are currently subject to a percent of value or a specific monetary amount, whichever is higher.

Temporary Imports
You can import goods for six months without payment if you have a bank guarantee stating that they will be used for exhibitions or demonstrations. If the product is not re-exported, you will be liable for duties and tax.

Customs Valuation
Customs valuation procedures may appear somewhat random because the import value of a good may fluctuate. In fact, the Customs Department keeps records of the highest declared prices of products imported into Thailand from invoices of previous

shipments and uses these "check prices" to assess tariffs on subsequent shipments of similar products from the same country.

Customs Department valuers may disregard actual invoiced values in favour of the check price—a practice which may affect agricultural products with seasonal prices. For products shipped from a country other than the country of origin, the Customs Department reserves the right to use the check price of the country of origin or the country of shipment, whichever is higher.

Import Documentation

An advance entry system has been implemented to assist importers, in which all documents may be submitted and processed prior to the arrival of goods. Upon arrival, only assessed duty and port charges remain to be paid.

The importation of foodstuffs presents special difficulties. Imported food items must be registered with the Thai Food and Drug Agency, which at times can be a painstaking and time-consuming task.

Labels must be registered with the Thai Food and Drug Administration and affixed to food products imported for sale in Thailand. Labels must identify, in the Thai language, the product

---

Importing Cosmetics—An Example

A product controlled by the Food and Drug Administration is cosmetics. Under the Cosmetic Act (B.E. 2517) of 1974, both the method of analysis of the product and the data establishing consumer benefit must be submitted to the Thai FDA for approval. Controlled cosmetics are also subject to product registration besides normal licensing requirements. To secure an import permit, product samples, quantitative formulae, a notarised/legalised letter guaranteeing compliance with the Thai cosmetics regulations, and identification of preservatives must be submitted to the Thai FDA.

Source: CIA Report, 1994

name, its weight or volume, its expiry or manufacture date and a general description of the product. Any food used by restaurateurs must also have the names and addresses of the manufacturer and distributor, as well as the registration number. Alcohol need not be labelled in Thai.

Export Controls
Restrictions on exports include products that involve environmental degradation (teak, ivory, and endangered animal and bird species and products), cultural concerns (Buddha images and antiques), and national security and sustenance (maintaining adequate supplies of staples, e.g. rice, to feed the Thai people). Exports may also be restricted by trade agreements such as international commodity agreements, agreements governing the textile and apparel trade, agreements on subsidies, and anti-dumping treaties.

In general, Thailand is anxious to promote exports and will make every effort to help the manufacturer.

Export Documentation
Customs procedures require the submission of an export entry form, along with several other documents (invoice, packing list, bill of lading, letter of credit), to the customs officer.

Other Trade Barriers
Non-tariff barriers exist to hamper the smooth passage of imports into the country. Many importers feel that the Customs Department's procedures are a barrier to trade because of demands for unrecorded cash at each step of the clearance procedure.

Among the barriers to exports are unreliable delivery of goods, and slow and insecure transportation inside the country.

Perhaps the most imposing barriers to both import and investment in Thailand are the complicated specifications regulating foreign ownership and control of companies, which have been covered in some detail earlier in this chapter.

Quality Standards

Goods made in Thailand have developed a reputation for poor quality in some markets. Very few Thai companies meet the ISO 9000 series of standards, which is the international standard for quality in design, production, installation and service of finished goods. In addition to international standards, Thailand has its own national standards authority, Thailand Industrial Standard (TIS)

Intellectual Property

Thailand is aware of the problems of intellectual property protection and has agreed to police its existing laws against intellectual theft. Its aim is to bring copyright agreements in line with the Uruguay Round agreements and the Berne Convention. However, this objective had still not been accomplished in 1997.

The 1992 amendments to the Trademark Act impose higher penalties for infringement and extend protection to service, certification and collective marks. Trademarks registered in Thailand receive protection for a term of 10 years and registration can be extended for an unlimited number of additional 10-year periods. Infringement remains a serious problem, with copycat brands being a major problem. One shopper commented that the quality of the copycat brands improved the closer she was to the originating shop, so that by the time she reached the designer shop, she was uncertain as to the authenticity of the goods in it!

The Copyright Act of 1978 provides a term of protection extending 50 years after the death of the creator. However, the 1978 law grants no explicit protection for computer software. It also contains broad exceptions permitting copying and provides minimal penalties for piracy. The activity in photocopying shops before the start of each university term suggests that copyright is not taken seriously—at least not by students.

Thailand's Efforts at Tackling Piracy of Intellectual Property (An International View)
In 1993, the US Trade Department placed Thailand on a "Priority Watch List" pending the completion of improvements to the legal regime. Today, Thailand is still on the list, indicating that the US Trade Department has yet to be satisfied with Thailand's performance in protecting the integrity of intellectual property.

A 1997 report noted that the principal economic disagreements between the United States and Thailand are:

- Arbitrary custom valuation procedures
- Insufficient protection of intellectual property rights

Other nations hold the same concerns.

The government has proposed setting up an intellectual property court so that disputes can be handled more efficiently.

According to the US Trade Estimate Report on foreign trade barriers, to date, no one in Thailand has ever served time in prison for copyright piracy or trademark counterfeiting. The report claims that fines are too low to deter offenders and that illicit goods continue to be sold at the retail level. The 1997 raid on shops in Panthip Plaza—the computer hardware and software centre of Bangkok—and the seizure of millions of dollars' worth of pirated materials may be a sign that the government is beginning to implement the existing counterfeit laws.

Protection for overseas copyright, patent and trademark holders remains a prominent issue in Thailand's relationship with trading partners, particularly the United States. Foreign firms should protect their intellectual property rights by registering their patents and trademarks. Lawyers specialised in intellectual property protection can be also be hired to take legal action to suppress piracy, although this can be a lengthy process.

Summary

Establishing a business in Thailand is more straightforward now than it ever was. The Thai economy needs foreign capital and foreign expertise to weather the current economic crisis.

The rules for starting a business in Thailand are no more daunting than they are in any other country. Some of the bureaucratic procedures may seem conservative but with careful attention to detail and the guidance of an interpreter, most bureaucratic red tape can be overcome.

The arbitrary assigning of specific areas with different incentives may seem unnecessary, but the zones and industrial estate network has been set up to move industry away from the (environmentally) least attractive areas towards the outer regions of Thailand where development is needed.

Following the Thai way will ensure that you take advantage of the incentives and avoid the problems associated with setting up a business in Thailand.

CHAPTER 6

Running the Business

Your approach to running a business in Thailand will depend on its nature. If you are an importer, despite the restrictions on imports, you will have a marketing advantage because of the Thai preference for foreign brands. However, you will be faced with the problem of decreasing disposable income and increased local competition as the "Buy Thai" campaign picks up pace. As an exporter you will have the advantage of full government support but will need to deal with the problems of Thai bureaucracy. If you are a consultant, manager, manufacturer or service supplier, you may face the problem of dealing with local staff who follow different procedures from those you take for granted.

Marketing

Strategy

Foreign firms marketing their products in Thailand should stress the quality of their goods and dissociate themselves from the products of NICs. Thai customers expect foreign products to be stylish, well designed, periodically improved and more reliable than local products. However, this preference for foreign goods may be reversed with the "Buy Thai" campaign that is under way.

Get a local agent or an expatriate who has a good working knowledge of the dos and don'ts of Thai society to prepare your marketing campaign. You will need a person to advise you on how quickly a campaign can be put together and what problems to expect with the campaign.

Product Knowledge

Exporters to Thailand should ensure that the local distribution agent understands their goods. Exporters should visit Thailand often and meet with their local agent and customers to enhance the working relationship. Thais value face-to-face, person-to-person contact to a much greater degree than people in the West.

Frequent visits will make you aware of the popularity of your products, and the progress and success of the marketing campaign. Your contact with Thailand will be difficult: verbal conversation may be difficult and written communication, while more secure and more accurately understood, may not be answered. If you are not getting a reply to your mail, it could be that your Thai agent does not understand your question and would rather lose business than lose face by asking you for clarification. Another reason could be that the Thai agent never received your mail.

Or it could be an entirely different problem. Finding out what is really going on with your Thai business colleague can be one of your greatest challenges and visiting Thailand to find out exactly what is going on can be one of your greatest pleasures.

Another approach is to invite Thai representatives to visit your domestic operations. This will be interpreted as an honour and may give you the opportunity to explain how your product works. Alternatively, you could send reliable foreign staff to work with the Thai representative and provide assistance in training and sales. This is one of the best ways to keep track of your business but take care to brief your staff thoroughly before sending them to the "land of smiles"—you do not want them to make the vital mistake of trying to change the entire Thai culture in order to do things "the way they are done back home".

Advertising and Promotions

Advertising expenditure in Thailand has increased much faster than the overall rate of economic growth. From 1979 to 1995, the average annual growth rate in advertising revenue was a staggering 23%.

National Expenditure on Advertising (million baht)				
Year	TV	Papers	Others	Total
1979	667	267	633	1,557
1985	2,729	1,097	1,521	5,348
1990	6,502	3,620	3,390	13,513
1995	18,663	11,771	11,798	41,234

Advertising is an important investment in Thailand. Newspaper, television and radio advertising space as well as billboards are available for your use. Censorship of advertisements is thorough—nudity is not allowed and royalty is not even alluded to in any advertisement. Some local advertisements are moralistic—a popular advertisement in 1997 featured a rich businessman being reprimanded by the ghost of his mother when he wasted food in a restaurant.

Check carefully to make sure that you are not being culturally offensive. A recent Airwalk advertisement featuring a monk wearing sports shoes caused a strong reaction in Thailand although it was aired only in the United States. Public reaction was so strong that the advertisement was withdrawn and an apology sent to the Thai Embassy in Washington.

Brochures are another avenue for publicity. Problems arise if you intend to produce only English language material. Firstly, they cannot reach the large non-English-speaking Thai audience. Secondly, for English language brochures containing technical information, your customer might be stumped by the technicality of the content even if he or she can read English better than speak it. It is, therefore, a good idea to have bilingual brochures, or two sets of brochures—one in English and one in Thai.

Another problem with technical content is that Thai is essentially a nontechnical language, so few brochures on technical and engineering products are translated into the Thai language.

Billboard advertising is a popular form of publicity in Thailand.

In fact, technicians and engineers actually work with a combination of Thai and English, where important words are translated into Thai but the bulk of the technical jargon remain in English.

It is important to make sure that your agent understands the brochure and your product. Most Thai agents are reluctant to ask questions as it may reveal their ignorance. The only way to check whether your agent or importer really understands the finer points of your product is to establish it during a personal visit.

Exhibitions, conventions, tours, and other promotions that offer people a chance to meet and talk about your products are good ideas—though costly ones. Trade fairs, education exhibits and seminars that teach people how to use a product (for example, language courses or computer software packages) are also popular. Convention centres and hotels offer several packages, which they tailor to your needs, at competitive prices.

There are also several occasions in each calendar year for the distribution of promotional material. New Year calendars are popular in Thailand, as are diaries, pens and umbrellas, all of which should display your logo.

Media Choices

Television Television advertisements are effective. Although not all families own a television set, most Thais watch television some time during the day—in a mall, shop or restaurant. Prices are competitive with other forms of media—a 30-second television spot will cost less than a full page newspaper advertisement.

Radio Radio programming is similar to Western countries—music, talk shows and lots of advertisements. In Bangkok, there is even a 24-hour talkback radio station dedicated entirely to reporting city traffic snarls. Taxi drivers switch from this channel to other more interesting channels as they navigate the best path to reach your destination. Whatever else they are doing, Thais like background noise—be it music or traffic jam reports—so radio is a good vehicle for publicity.

Newspaper A choice of Thai, English and Chinese language newspapers is available for advertising and publicity. There is also a growing number of specialist magazines, which cater to almost every market niche.

Proofread all advertisements that you plan to submit in English—some of the errors are lamentable while others are misleading. Though your agency will translate your English and Chinese advertisements for you, ask a friend to check them if you do not know the languages.

Cinema Cinemas are state-of-the-art and great advertising venues, especially if you are trying to reach a young market. Thais love the cinema—the more special effects, the better— and Hollywood blockbusters invariably draw huge crowds. Most modern Thai films are low budget action movies that feature young actresses and actors, romance, ripped bodices, tears and violence.

Public Relations

Most companies have well-staffed public relations offices. It is vitally important to train your public relations staff as fully as your sales people for they will be the ones handling enquiries.

Equally important is your network of contacts. All businesses in Thailand have extensive networks through social and business associations. Being a foreigner also attaches a certain amount of status to you. However, it is also important to attend the right meetings and to know people in your industry.

Labour Force

Size and Composition

In 1996, Thailand's total workforce was approximately 33 million. Roughly speaking, labour employment by sector was as follows: 58% in agriculture, 12 % in manufacturing and 30% in services.

There has recently been a labour drift from the rural areas to the cities, which the government is trying to stop through the implementation of a decentralisation policy. Unskilled workers are attempting to move into labour-intensive industries such as textiles, but employment in this industry is itself under threat from automation and foreign competition. In an attempt to increase productivity, the Thai Government has made improvements to the quality of its workforce one of its primary goals.

Nature

In job vacancy advertisements, knowledge of the English language is often listed as an essential criterion. Such a clause restricts your work pool to only middle-class graduates from the universities and colleges. Decide how much English your staff really needs to know if you are not employing them as technicians or clerks.

Many Thai men leave work for a period of time—ranging from days to months—to become monks.

Absenteeism is fairly high in Thailand, where employees may not have the dedication towards work that has come to be expected in some other countries. Most Thais have a series of obligations to carry out that are deemed more important than work. Male staff may leave work for indefinite periods of time to enter a monastery or to complete military training. Entering a monastery is voluntary and the period away from work can vary from days to months. These men soon return to work with a shaved head and resume work as if they had not been away.

Military training is compulsory for men over 21 years of age. A male staff member may be away for a week, a weekend, a month or longer, depending on how much service he did before he graduated from college. Such absences are fully sanctioned by the state and in some instances, the employer must keep paying the absent staff member.

Both men and women periodically leave their work to go upcountry to their hometowns for religious festivals and ceremonies such as Songkran and funerals, as well as to vote in their home constituencies at election time.

Wages
Labour costs in Thailand increased as the country developed over the past few years. Even so, labour costs in Thailand are still cheap by world standards, though not in all industries.

1996 Employment Costs for a Process Worker

Location	$US	Index
Osaka	33,348	1176
Los Angeles	30,979	1092
Seoul	24,529	865
Singapore	16,642	587
Hong Kong	16,335	576
Kuala Lumpur	5,223	184
Shanghai	3,520	124
Bangkok	**2,837**	**100**
Jakarta	2,362	83

Source: KPMG data

Note:
Cost of labour in this table covers all labour additives. Figures are in US$ per annum.

After adjustment for inflation, the real annual rise in the average income of Thai households was 10.3% between 1989 and 1990, 10.6% between 1990 and 1992, and 6.5% from 1992 to 1994. Statistics also show a growing disparity between urban and rural income.

The average wage per day is 146 baht, with a 2% rise forecast for 1998. Since 1990, when the average wage per day was 90 baht, the percentage increase each year has been higher than the cost

These workers are performing their daily duty of attaching roses to poles in the Rose Garden, a popular tourist attraction near Bangkok. Their work is meticulous, painstaking and repetitive. It is an extremely low-paid job.

of living, though the Internal Trade Department and the Bank of Thailand report different figures.

Unemployment

The unemployment rate is about 4% and is likely to increase as companies try to cut costs to meet competition from other NICs and the West, where robotisation is increasing. In addition, the recent economic slowdown will likely add accountants, journalists and other professionals to the ranks of the unemployed.

Wages are low and Thai companies employ labour fairly freely. For example, most companies' gates are permanently manned by two or three guards and offices are filled with people doing simple paperwork. Cashing a traveller's cheque or making a purchase in a department store also attracts the help of three or four people. As the country reacts to competition from neighbouring NICs, such employment practices must be re-examined.

Downsizing is not popular in Thailand. People are moved laterally or given a job they dislike. Employers hope that staff will choose to leave so that they can avoid paying the three months' wage that employees who are fired are entitled to.

However, competitive pressure may force a change in Thai business culture, which is already being eroded by foreign investment, and management and business practices. As Thailand finances its operations by importing debt and equity to higher degrees, more automation and staff cuts will follow. Also, Thai businesses now have to compete more aggressively to maintain their overseas market share due to the third wave of industrialisation—computerisation.

Western economies are becoming more competitive as they replace people with machines. Thailand, together with other NICs, will undoubtedly have to adopt automation and will inevitably experience the same impact on employment as some Western countries.

Trade Unions

Thailand is not a strongly unionised country and only about 1.2% of the labour force belongs to unions or state enterprise associations. There are about 600 private sector unions registered in Thailand, which are pushing to enhance the rights of workers. However, in light of the 1997 downturn, the issue of workers' rights is unlikely to top the government's reform agenda.

Union proposals to improve the lot of the working population include the following wish list. It is unlikely that any of the proposals will be implemented (with the exception of the last one).

The Trade Union Wish List

- Social security compensation by 1998
- Medical treatment for social security cardholders
- Nursery centres in all workplaces
- Making the labour relations law a subject in the high school level curriculum
- Abolition of the minimum wage and introduction of a workers' pay scale
- Controlling the price of consumer goods
- Affordable accommodation for workers
- Scrapping the privatisation plan for state enterprises
- Allowing state enterprise workers to set up unions
- Amendment of the election law to make migrant workers eligible to vote in the constituencies where their workplaces are located
- Protection of the rights of union founders and members
- The stepping up of efforts to trace labour leader Thanong Pho-an who disappeared in 1991
- Amendment of labour related laws to ensure fair treatment
- Allowing workers' representatives to sit on the tripartite committee of the Board of Investment and the Joint Public-Private Consultative Committee
- Controlling the influx of illegal workers

Labour Day demands, 1997

Labour Laws

Labour issues are regulated by the National Employment Code (NEC) Announcement 103 and the Labour Act (1975). The Civil and Commercial Code governs the termination of employment and its related consequences. Theoretically, Thais are guaranteed most of the internationally recognised worker rights, including the freedom of association in the private sector.

Conditions of Labour
The following conditions are part of the Announcement 103:

- The maximum number of hours per work week is 48 for industrial workers, 54 for clerical workers and 42 for workers in hazardous environments.
- Each worker is entitled to one hour's break after five hours of work.
- An employee is entitled to one day of leave per week (usually Sunday) and at least 13 traditional holidays per year, including National Labour Day.
- An employee is entitled to paid medical absences not exceeding 30 days per year. If an employee is absent for three or more consecutive days, he is obliged to submit a medical certificate, except in cases of emergency. Failure to do so may result in dismissal.
- An employee is entitled to take military leave when called to service by the government. However, the employer is not obliged to pay for his leave of absence beyond 60 days per year

  Further, Announcement 103 is regarded as a law of public order and morals; therefore employer and employee may not agree to alter the minimum standard it provides.

Laws passed are not always implemented. The minimum age for workers (13 years) is not always applied, nor are women always given the three months paid maternity leave (granted in 1993).

Wages and salaries are negotiated by individual firms. Industry-wide collective bargaining is unusual and workers for different car parts factories need not be paid the same rate. Relatively few work days are lost to strikes as the unions are not powerful. In 1993, 214,000 days were lost to strikes and the trend is towards fewer work day losses to labour strikes.

State enterprise workers, like civil servants, may not form unions but are allowed membership in employee associations. The law currently denies the right to strike to civil servants, state enterprise workers, and workers in essential services such as education, transportation and healthcare.

Redundancy

When it comes to protecting the interests of Thai labour, foreign businesses may be discriminated against. In 1997, the Labour and Social Welfare Ministry legislated to protect Thai employees from possible mass lay-offs by foreign companies (automation and other reasons were cited).

Cause and Effect of Unemployment
Cause: Loss of Jobs in the Textile Industry
Notices for mass lay-offs were put up at Thai American Textile and Thai Melon Textile. To allow management to introduce 100 new cloth-cutting machines, 740 workers were sacked.
(Source: *Bangkok Post*, 14 March 1997)

Effect: Protection of the Workforce
The Labour and Social Welfare Ministry has formed a committee to oversee the interests of Thai workers. Under this scheme, over 2,599 foreign-owned businesses nationwide will be watched by the proposed panel, which will be chaired by the deputy prime minister and will comprise 14 other representatives from relevant state agencies. The committee supplements the present labour laws, which are too inefficient to protect workers effectively.

However, protecting the rights of workers runs counter to some of the government's other economic objectives. In particular, the government is conscious of the competition that Thailand faces from its neighbours, such as Bangladesh, Burma, Laos, Cambodia, Vietnam and China, which have lower labour costs.

Health and Safety Laws

With reports of incidents such as collapsed multi-storey buildings and uncontrolled fires, unsafe bridges and toxic poisoning, Thailand has earned a reputation for having poor supervision of infrastructure quality, and lax safety laws.

The Royal Jomtien Fire
In July 1997, a fire started in the kitchen of the Royal Jomtien Hotel at Pattaya Beach. Aside from those who were rescued from the roof by helicopter, over 90 international and domestic guests perished in their rooms. It was later discovered that the hotel management had padlocked the fire escape to prevent people from escaping from the hotel without paying their bills.

Anyone who visits the country and stumbles on the broken footpaths of Bangkok will realise that quality control is not a high priority for the nation. Government supervision of infrastructure is almost nonexistent and standards have lapsed.

One of the government's economic objectives is to maintain the attractiveness of Thailand as an investment site by keeping the cost of labour down. Reports of industrial health hazards and unsafe practices are reported but are either dismissed or attributed to accidental causes. The most common way of dealing with a reported violation of health and safety regulations is to promise to investigate the matter—later.

The apparent disregard of safety laws by Thais is not a green light for the foreign investor to do the same. The rules are there

> **AIDS as an Industrial Accident**
> At the Northern Region Industrial Estate in 1994, 14 workers died of what was officially declared to be AIDS. In actual fact, the workers had died from exposure to manganese, lead and aluminium. In 1997, three more workers died, and hundreds of others fell ill and quit their jobs. These deaths were attributed to general illnesses. Doctors employed by the government were under instruction to avoid negative publicity that might adversely affect the activities of the company. None of the investigators indicated that metal poisoning had occurred.

and you, as the investor, may find yourself the target of legal action if you do not try to adhere to the codes.

Environmental Legislation

After decades of neglect, Thailand tightened its environmental legislation by declaring new environmental regulations in 1992. The legislation that embodied a new caring attitude to the environment was the Enhancement and Conservation Quality Act (1992). This legislation is based on the "polluter pays" principle. The act has also established new standards for industrial effluents, air emission and water quality.

Under the act, all proposed developments are subject to an Environmental Impact Study that must be first approved by the Ministry of Science, Technology and Environment.

The act recognises an increase in third party rights. Under the act, anyone who believes himself or herself affected by the project is entitled to question the ministry regarding the proposed development. Individuals have the right to file complaints directly against polluters and seek remedies for environmental damage caused by the development. At the same time, penalties for violating environmental regulations were increased, and today, polluters face heavy penalties. Penalties are imposed, not only on the polluting corporation, but also on responsible individuals within the offending corporation such as the managing director.

Environment—Changing Attitudes

Other indications that the government may at last be getting serious about protecting the environment include the 1996 shutdown of the Phoenix Pulp and Paper Company for dumping untreated waste into the Ping River. The six-week shutdown cost the company $2.5 million in cleanup costs and lost revenue.

For a significant change to happen in the country as a whole, however, past environmental transgressions would have to be addressed. In dealing with environmental issues, as in other areas, government action is often hampered by conflicts of interest between members of the government and their business interests.

Environmental conflicts in Thailand are often between individuals and companies. For this reason, legislation is not always applied and there have been cases where complainants have been bought off with cash to drop their complaints.

Taxation

Thailand has a relatively small tax burden at both the individual and corporate level. The Department of Revenue is not yet fully-computerised and there is no complete list of all taxpaying citizens. Investigations of the "unusually rich", whose assets far outweigh their earning capacity and whose source of wealth is supposedly illegal, usually end with the resignation of the investigator.

Personal Income Tax

Income tax is levied on assessable income earned in Thailand. It includes the payment for employment plus income earned from investments and other pecuniary activity within the kingdom. Assessable income will be taxed at progressive rates scheduled in

---

Corruption in the Tax Office
IBM worked with the tax department in Thailand to institute a computerised taxation system that would issue each citizen with an identifying tax number. However, the objectives of this programme were frustrated, possibly by government officials with a vested interest in keeping the business affairs of wealthy friends and relatives undisclosed. IBM invested millions of dollars in the project but finally admitted defeat. It left the project in mid-1997.

---

the code. Compared to most other countries, income tax in Thailand is not high—about 10% for a median range income.

Corporate Income Tax
Companies, registered ordinary partnerships, limited partnerships and joint ventures are called "juristic persons" in Thai legalese. The net profits of corporations are subject to income tax. This constitutes all revenue arising from or in connection with the business carried out in the accounting period—after the deduction of all expenses in the manner prescribed by Thai legislated accounting standards.

Value Added Tax (VAT)
On 1 January 1992, the government replaced all previous taxes on business inputs and outputs with the VAT on end sale value, eliminating multiple taxation. Taxes are collected for the sale of goods and services at every stage of production and are assessed at three rates depending on the total revenue of the business being taxed. Revenue between 600,000 and 1.2 million baht pays a VAT of 1.5%. For revenue over 1.2 million baht, the VAT is 10%. Businesses below 600,000 baht are tax exempt. Check the current scale for your tax rate.

VAT at each stage is added by the seller and is collected through the production chain until the final sale to the individual consumer. The final seller of the goods is required to calculate, collect and remit the VAT to the government.

All good and services sold inside the kingdom and all goods imported into the kingdom are subject to VAT according to the Revenue Code. Even a foreign company operating in Thailand through an agent is subject to tax.

Exemptions from VAT

By royal decree, a number of businesses are exempt from VAT. Such businesses include, amongst others, banking, finance, securities, life insurance, pawnshops and real estate.

In addition, businesses and goods that would normally attract VAT may also be exempt by virtue of where the goods and services will be sold. Exempted from VAT are:

- All exported goods and services
- Goods and/or services sold to government agencies or state enterprises

The refund from the government is extremely slow because of the amount of paperwork generated and possibly, the government's cash flow difficulties. Refund of VAT on exported goods may take as long as seven to 10 months, a delay which exporters have protested against.

Stamp Duty

Stamp duty is a tax imposed on documents and is collected at the rate specified in the Stamp Duty Schedule of the Revenue Code. Stamp duty is payable on most contracts and leases. The Revenue Code designates the person in charge of affixing and cancelling the stamp duty.

Any document on which insufficient duty has been paid becomes inadmissible in court. All contracts and leases should have a complete stamp duty attached to it at the time of its execution.

Contracting parties residing outside Thailand are given 30 days to get the stamp attached.

Repatriation of Profit

Through the Exchange Control Act of 1942 (as amended), the Bank of Thailand maintained its international commitment to facilitate free trade through the free flow of capital.

There is no restriction on the amount of foreign currency that may be brought into the country but what foreign currency is brought in must be sold to an authorized agent or deposited into a foreign currency deposit account within 15 days of the arrival date. There are, however, exceptions to this rule, for example, it does not apply to travellers passing through Thailand, foreign embassies and international organisations. Purchase of foreign bank notes and coins within Thailand is unrestricted if the money is used for travelling or business purposes.

Thai residents who make foreign investments or loans to their affiliated companies overseas in amounts exceeding US$5 million per year require prior approval. Remittance for purchase of immovable property (land or houses) or securities in a foreign country also requires prior approval, regardless of the amount.

Foreign Currency Deposit Account

Thai citizens and corporations are permitted to open a foreign currency deposit account under the following conditions:

- The account must be opened with a commercial bank in Thailand.
- The total balance at any one time should not exceed US$500,000 for a natural person and US$5 million for a corporation.
- Foreign currency in the account must be derived from abroad.
- Thai citizens and Thai corporations may make withdrawals from the accounts for normal business transactions to persons outside the country upon submission of supporting documents.

Non-resident Baht Account

A non-resident baht account is an account opened by a foreign person not residing in Thailand. This account can be operated normally and attracts the normal rate of interest paid to Thai residents. However, there is no particular advantage to having a separate account in Thailand when money can be transferred easily though satellite systems.

Summary

The mechanics of starting, owning and running a business are complicated. The main factors that make running a business more difficult in Thailand include the need for a new marketing strategy, an unfamiliar labour force, different laws and of course, language differences. Being aware of these difficulties is halfway to overcoming them.

Operating your business the Thai way is a day-to-day exercise in combining two different cultures and can lead to problems that make the mechanics of setting up and running a business seem difficult. The chapters entitled "The Thai Way" and "Communicating at Work" explain some of the work patterns and communication problems that can occur. These chapters also offer advice on how to deal with them.

CHAPTER 7

The Thai Way

The Thai way is the belief in, and the respect for, the destined order of things. As such, Thailand has a strong social hierarchy. The different groups or influences within the hierarchy are:

- The Buddhist monks
- The king and the royal family
- The military, who have historically held most of the power in the country
- The Chinese who manage the trade and money industries in the country
- Public servants
- The growing middle class
- Farmers and labourers, and their dependants—the biggest group in the population

The duties and obligations imposed on an individual from his or her position in the social hierarchy has important implications for business in Thailand. If any conflict of interest arises between a Thai's social obligations and work obligations, his or her social obligations always come first.

As the Thai social structure is based on Buddhism, your working life might not be affected drastically if your staff is predominantly Christian or Muslim. However, as Buddhism is the main religion in Thailand, you will almost certainly encounter it in your daily life.

To what extent the Thai social attitudes will affect your business depends very much on the nature of your business, the number of Thais on your staff, the location of your company—whether it is upcountry or in the city—and so on.

Buddhist Influences

Life and Buddhist Philosophy

"In the past five decades, Thailand has confronted numerous problems, from poverty, political instability, weak democratic governments, dishonesty of public figures, to the communist threat. Nonetheless, Thailand has cut through those obstacles and dealt with the problems with a certain degree of success. Adherence to the middle way of moderation, perseverance, tolerance of differences and adaptation has been its strength."

— From the speech entitled "The 21st Century: The Rise of Asia" by H.E. Gen. Prem Tinsulanonda, former prime minister of Thailand, on 26 November 1996.

General Prem's comment that adherence to "the middle way" has helped solve Thailand's problems reflects the influence of Buddhism in Thailand. "The middle way" keeps Thais on a path between extremes in life and reduces conflicts. Thais who adhere to Buddhist teachings are much respected in society.

Two of the main teachings in Thai Buddhism are the belief in rebirth, whereby every life, human or animal, is only a phase in a cycle of innumerable lives and the belief in karma, whereby every good or bad deed brings about an appropriate consequence either in the present life or in some future life. The belief that things will work out in the next life if not in this one and that you will eventually be rewarded or punished for whatever you do stems from these beliefs.

These personal beliefs help Thais accept their place in the hierarchy of both life and work.

The Office Blessing Ceremony

When a new company opens its doors, the standard practice is to have Buddhist monks bless the new premises. This consists of an elaborate ceremony of chanting and praying performed by several monks from the local monastery, after which there will be much feasting and celebrating.

Thais believe that the blessing ceremony contributes significantly to the success of a business. Whether you agree or not, there is not much harm in allowing the ceremony to go ahead anyway. For a start, it could prevent your staff from putting the blame on you if anything goes wrong in the future. More importantly, the ceremony shows your willingness to do things the Thai way and will undoubtedly increase the esteem that staff have for you and your business.

The ceremony will always take place in the morning as monks are forbidden to eat after 12 noon. The date of your office blessing ceremony will be set by the abbot from the temple in accordance with astrological calculations.

On the day of the blessing ceremony, provisions will have to be made to transport the monks to the office premises and a room will have to be prepared—it should be large enough for the monks and staff to sit on the floor. When the monks arrive, you will be the first in line to *wai* the monks if you are the company head, followed by the rest of your staff (the *wai* is a well-known Thai greeting; see chapter 8 for a more detailed explanation). The monks will then sit in line in front of the staff and chant for about half an hour. When this is over, the monks will give their blessing by sprinkling water over the staff as well as the office premises.

The office personnel will now serve the food to the monks, starting with the abbot. If you are the head of the company, you will have the honour of being the first to serve the food. When serving, do not fill the monks' bowls to the brim. Remember that your staff are close behind you and want to give their respects to the monks as well

Women cannot give food directly to a monk. Place food carefully in the bowl without touching it or have a man hand it to the monk on your behalf.

Once the monks have departed, give your staff time to enjoy lunch with the food remaining from the ceremony—remember that Thais enjoy food and fun every now and then.

The manager's main role, apart from participating in the blessing, is to pay for the event—the main expenses being food and a donation to the monk's temple.

Do not worry that you might make a mistake that will hurt the Thais' sensibilities. Somebody among your staff will usually know the ropes and can guide you along.

Time from Work

The Thais follow the lunar calendar so the three major religious festivals are tied to the full moon in the months of February, May and July. The traditional Thai new year is tied to the full moon in April and the charming festival of Loy Kratong is a November full moon festival. During these holidays, Thai staff will usually return to their hometowns

As mentioned in chapter 6, men may take time off during this period to enter a monastery to "make merit".

Spirit Houses

If your staff requests it, install a spirit house when you start your business and have it blessed.

These decorative shrines are more a result of animism than of Buddhism as the house is thought to act as a home for the spirits dispossessed by your building. The spirit house is usually erected towards the front of or in a visible corner of your location. If your company has an office within a larger building, the landlord would normally provide a spirit house specifically for your business.

You will notice that as staff arrive at work, they may *wai* the spirit house. It also acts as a place to make offerings and prayers, and staff will often leave garlands of flowers and burning incense after doing so. A Buddha image is often included in the shrine.

Most spirit houses and shrines are garlanded with flowers and other offerings. Thai staff also offer incense daily as a sign of respect.

Superstitions

Apart from spirit houses and the belief in auspicious dates for office blessing ceremonies and the like, Thais have a lot of superstitions that might affect business. For example, the Thai finance minister resigned in June 1997 when the Thai economy was going through tough times. When this happened, some parliamentarians said (and really believed) that the two large wooden elephants standing at the doors of the Finance Ministry were cursed and had jinxed the minister, causing the country's economic problems. In the same vein, a Buddha image kept at Lang Suan police station was thought to have brought misfortune—culminating in the murder-suicide of six officers in 1997. Stories of good luck charms and rites, and of bad luck aversion exist side by side with Buddhism.

Sometimes, Thai staff will visit a professional astrologer for assistance when making business or personal decisions. Until recently, most hairdressers closed on a Wednesday because of the Brahman belief that it is bad luck to cut hair on this day!

Royal Influences

Most offices prominently display a portrait of the Thai king and queen. Next to Buddhism, the monarchy is the most profoundly influential institution in Thailand. There is even a special language used only to address the royal family.

The Thai constitution states that nothing derogatory shall be said about the king or members of the royal family. If you were to express a negative opinion, a Thai would see this as a display of your ignorance of Thailand and not as an indication that there is anything wrong with the monarchy.

It is worth noting that unlike other countries, where the media is free to broadcast negative publicity on the royal family, nothing of the sort will ever happen in Thailand. The monarchy is treated with the utmost respect. For example, defacing a bank note or coin would be seen as an insult to the monarchy as both display the king's portrait.

When visiting movie theatres in Thailand, remember to stand with the rest of the audience when the king's anthem is played and portraits of the king are projected on the movie screen before the start of the main feature.

The king's birthday in December is a national holiday and the queen's birthday in August is celebrated as Mother's Day. The queen also presides at the Trooping of the Colours and the king officiates at merit making ceremonies honouring past kings such as Chulalongkorn, whose holiday is observed in October.

However, even though the royal family is at the pinnacle of social life in Thailand, we have seen in the introduction to this chapter that the king and his family still have to show respect to Buddhist monks, who are at the top of the Thai social hierarchy.

Military Influences

The military was organised by past kings to protect Thailand against its neighbours and had access to organisational strategies and education long before the rest of the population. It sponsored the coup against the monarchy in 1932 and has been active in politics ever since. However, its power seems to be waning, as more middle-ranking officers retire early to join the private sector rather than carry on until the age of 60 and a previously assured rank of general.

However, the military still has a role in politics and business. The military budget is the third highest, only lagging behind that of the Ministry of the Interior and the Ministry of Education. Both regular and retired military officers form part of the appointed Senate. Thailand's elected prime minister in 1996, Chavalit Yongchaiyudh, was a former army general who also held the post of defence minister. The last (elected) prime minister without a military background was Chatichai Choonhavan who came to power in 1988.

Retired and active senior military officers are found in many state-owned enterprises, particularly those dealing with aviation and maritime affairs. Until 1992, all the chairpersons of the national carrier, Thai Airways International, were officials of the Royal Thai Air Force.

As mentioned earlier, all men must serve time in the army and the option is open for students to become cadets in high school. Some men on your staff will have to take time off to fulfil military obligations. You will be expected to accept their absence and to pay them for up to 60 days of their service.

Chinese Influences

Despite making up only 10% of the national population of 60 million, the Chinese in Thailand wield significant control over the private sector. They control four of the five largest banks in Thailand, which handle 50% of Thailand's GDP. Thailand's largest bank, the Bangkok Bank, is also the largest in Southeast Asia.

The Chinese in Thailand have been estimated to own at least 50% of all investments in the banking and finance sector, and 90% of all investments in the manufacturing and commercial sectors. These are impressive figures considering that most Chinese were driven by poverty from their homelands to find a better life in Thailand.

That the Chinese make up 10% of the population is only an approximate figure at best. The Chinese have been in Thailand a long time and have assimilated successfully into Thai culture. In fact, there are not many Thais today who do not have some Chinese blood. In the same vein, there are not many Chinese Thais today that have no Thais in their lineage.

The majority of Chinese in Thailand are Teochews originating from Hong Kong and Shantou (Swatow) in Guangdong Province, China. They owe their rise in Siam to King Taksin, a son of a Teochew businessman, who reunited Siam after Burmese invaders sacked the ancient capital Ayutthaya in 1767. King Taksin surrounded himself with Teochew advisers and the Teochew gradually gained high positions in Siam's aristocracy, government, commerce and industry. Over time, their presence grew.

In the early 1900s, King Rama VI commanded courtiers with Chinese blood to move to one side of the throne room—90% of the courtiers moved in accordance with the king's instructions.

The Thais have coexisted with the overseas Chinese in remarkable harmony. Instead of attempting to replace the Chinese in the economical or political arenas, the Thai Government realised that it would be more practical and beneficial to the nation as a whole to initiate cooperation with the Chinese in developing the Thai economy.

The Thai-Chinese subscribe fully to mainstream Thai values. Most of them, particularly those of the third generation or so, now consider themselves very much "Thai". They speak perfect Thai, eat Thai food and struggle to obtain an education in the best Thai universities.

Do not expect the Thai-Chinese, born and educated in Thailand, to behave like their distant ethnic cousins in Hong Kong or Beijing, though many Thai-Chinese maintain Chinese religions and traditions. Alongside Buddha statues, the Thai-Chinese staff may have pictures of Chinese gods and ancestors in their homes. They usually ask for time off during the Chinese New Year (around mid-February) and will eat only vegetarian food during the Vegetarian Festival in October. To some extent, the rest of Thailand joins in these celebrations, particularly Chinese New Year, when you will see a lot of the department stores decorated in red, the Chinese colour for celebration and prosperity.

Some Thai-Chinese staff may use a Chinese name at home and speak a Chinese dialect with their parents. Some Thai-Chinese have a different attitude to work from indigenous Thais. They have a high respect for education and put emphasis on entrepreneurship, flexibility and hard work. Most dream of one day owning their own business.

Profiles of Leading Chinese Business People

Chin Sophonpanich   He founded The Bangkok Bank in 1944. It has since become the largest bank in Thailand, with 344 branches. It is also the largest bank in Southeast Asia, with assets totalling US$8 billion (1991). Chin was born in the floating market of Bangkok and received his schooling in Shantou, China. Of the 1,200 largest businesses in Thailand, the Sophonpanich family is known to control at least 22 other companies listed. Chin passed away in 1988, leaving the family business with his six sons. Today, his eldest son manages the family's interests in Hong Kong, including the Commercial Bank of Hong Kong. His second son, Chatri, manages the Bangkok Bank.

Banthoon Lamsam   Born in Bangkok in 1953 and educated at Princeton and Harvard, Banthoon was appointed president of the Thai Farmers Bank in 1992 by his father, Bancha, who died some months later. The Lamsam family controls the Thai Farmers Bank and Loxley (Bangkok), and is considered one of the most influential families in Thailand. Other investments are in food and oil.

Dhanin Chearavanont   Dhanin and his family moved to Thailand from Guangdong Province in China in the 1920s, and opened a humble family store. In the 1950s, he set up Chareon Pokaphand (CP), a chicken feed mill. Today, CP is highly diversified with 200 companies, 49 of which are in China. TelecomAsia, a joint venture between CP Group and Nynex Ltd from the United States, is listed on Bangkok's stock exchange. After years of prosperity in Thailand, CP Group is now investing in China and in 1997, it had 130 joint ventures there.

Thaksin Shinawatra was born in 1949 in Chiang Mai in northern Thailand and was educated in the United States. He established the Shinawatra Computer and Communications Group in 1983 after resigning from the police force, where he had attained the rank of lieutenant colonel and had been put in charge of the Police Computer Centre. The company has since expanded from computers into telecommunications, cable TV, mobile telephones, paging systems and broadcasting which includes data services. Thaksin led the Palang Dharma Party briefly but resigned shortly after the November 1996 general election.

Chuan Leekpai and **Banharn Silpa-archa**   These are two recent prime ministers of Thailand also of Chinese descent.

Rural Influences

Thailand has always been an agricultural society and particularly in parts of northern and north eastern Thailand, life follows a traditional rural pattern. However, as Bangkok becomes more and more a focus of the Thai economy, it becomes a magnet for people living in the rural areas. The upcountry population is increasingly becoming educated in Bangkok schools, colleges and universities, and finding employment in its numerous factories and commercial firms. They bring with them their dialects, their culture, and more significantly to the foreign investor, their way of work.

Culture Shock
Newcomers to Thailand might be perplexed by some of the behaviours that Thai staff exhibit. In Thailand, you might even hear yourself exclaiming in exasperation and confusion:

"My staff have been aware for two weeks that our company is having problems meeting a delivery deadline. I find out about this the day before delivery."

"Every time I look up from my desk all my staff appear to be doing is chatting and eating snacks all day."

The root to the Thai's unique work culture lies in their rural culture. Take the time to understand what brings about such behaviour and you will better understand their way of working.

Work and leisure in the provinces evolve around well-defined climatic, religious and farming seasons. Planning ahead seems pointless as planting and harvesting times cannot be changed. Time is not viewed as linear and unidirectional as in the West, but as an infinite cycle of seasons. If a farmer and his wife miss this year's village festival, there is always next year or the year after that. The flip side of this apparent indifference to deadlines is the Thais' ability to work practically nonstop when it is vital to do so.

For the Thais, fun and cooperation are very much interrelated with work, an attitude that they carry to Bangkok. The word for work in Thai language is *ngarn*, which is also the word for a celebration, a festivity or a social function. So to the Thai, for example, the words labour, temple fair, birthday party and employment all mean the same thing—*ngarn*.

Farmers often help one another so that they will not be excluded from future group activities. From this need to work cooperatively has grown the tradition of *krengjai*, an extreme reluctance to impose on anyone or upset anyone by direct criticism, challenge or confrontation.

The provincial village is led by an elected headman, or *phu-yai-baan*, who is part of the provincial governing body. Until 1983, the *phu-yai-baan* was always a man. Though women are not prohibited from being the head of a village, reaching equality of opportunity has been slow. By 1997, less than 2% of village heads were women. The village hierarchy mentality is carried to the office, as is the attitude of the secondary role of women.

Comments about the availability of food are incorporated in Thai greetings. Thais will often remark on how "thin" or "fat" you look. This remark finds its origins in the gesture of friendship in rural villages, where food is not always available. However, it can be disconcerting, when you return to work after a holiday or an illness, to be greeted by "You've gained (lost) weight"!

Kinship

The basic unit of rural life in Thailand is the extended family, in which the father is regarded as the head. Women usually do the household chores and work in the fields during the planting and harvesting seasons. Men perform heavy tasks like the more strenuous field work. With several generations living under one roof, there is a lot less privacy in Thai homes than those in the West.

Caring for children is a shared responsibility among parents, grandparents and elder cousins. Children are assigned certain duties according to age and ability and as they grow older, their responsibilities increase. They are allowed to participate in family discussions, where their opinions are taken into account when important decisions are made.

In the workplace, the same delineation of duties occurs. Thai staff are not flexible or multi-tasked and they want a specialised job that is theirs alone. They also expect to be taught the ropes as they work. For instance, men arriving from upcountry will drive taxis though they are completely unfamiliar with the roads in the city. They assume that they will learn on the job—and they do.

Children are also taught to respect their elders at a very early age. They are aware of their positions in the family hierarchy, which is very important in Thai rural society. This habit of deference to elders makes Thais reluctant to oppose or otherwise confront a senior in the workplace.

Hierarchy in the Office

The Thai Social Hierarchy

The West professes to believe that all people are created equal and have equal opportunities. The social structure of such a society is flatter than that in Thailand, which is made up of an ordered series of classes. In Thailand, the only way to succeed in your business is to observe the rules of hierarchy.

A strong sense of hierarchy allows Thais to identify where they and others fit into the social system. Someone of a low social class will usually not challenge a decision or complain about his or her difficult situation. Such an attitude of fortitude stems from the Buddhist belief in karma, where one's destiny is predetermined.

To make clear a person's position in society, visible status symbols are used. Expensive jewellery, fancy cars, mobile phones, designer clothes, embossed business cards, good manners—these are all clear indications of the high position that a person has in society. Thais place much emphasis on dressing, on showing respect to other people and on behaving correctly to show one's social status.

When one of the foreign embassies in Bangkok held a National Day celebration, the ambassador decided to project a friendly image and dressed down for the event. The strategy did not work. It merely embarrassed the Thais of high social rank who attended the evening celebration only to see their host sloppily dressed.

At the workplace, it is essential to provide symbols and patterns that are familiar and recognisable to your staff if you expect good performance.

Titles

Thais keep any titles that they might once have had. For example, Thai businessmen who have retired from the military retain their title for use in public circles and some Thais hold other high status positions in addition to their full-time business positions, such as former professorship at leading universities. A Thai's status does not change as he moves from one role to another. Former titles and honours are simply added to his or her current position.

Timely promotions and thus, better titles, can increase staff morale and helps retain good staff who may have considered resigning. Conversely, a person can be forced to leave if demoted.

A fancy business card is also important. A card that shows the position of Head of Cash Receipts Department, for example, is preferred to one pronouncing a person to be just an Assistant Accountant. Such fancy titles are likely to allow your staff to open more doors to important contacts for your business. Access to people with power and influence is often more important to the Thai than their proven track record and professionalism.

Status of Managers

The Thai office hierarchy puts you on a higher status than you may have been used to at home. You will be responsible for more decision-making than you are accustomed to as Thai staff will usually not take the initiative. They feel that the taking of initiatives is the domain of the boss because of his or her education and experience. Thai staff are also reluctant to suggest new ideas as they consider it a sign of showing off. The creation of an environment where employees are empowered to take the initiative without censure from others may take time and effort. Consult your staff for their opinions although the final decision will ultimately be yours.

If you feel a communication barrier between you and your staff or if you feel that they are being too deferential to you, make a special effort to remember their names. Most Thais have first names, which are long and difficult to pronounce. They will be delighted to know that you have made the effort to cross the language barrier. Most Thais have shorter nicknames, which you may prefer to use once your subordinates have warmed to you.

Caring for your staff is very important as the manager in Thailand carries a great degree of responsibility for the personal lives of his subordinates. For example, a manager will often discuss the employees' personal life with them to make sure everything is running smoothly at home. Such shows of concern demonstrate the manager's supportive role towards the employees.

The Thai way is to respond to a manager who is friendly and shows he cares. Such a manager is paternal and all-knowing, and at the same time, does not cause anyone to "lose face". This style is wonderful for relationships but it can also impede productivity and prevent you from achieving your objectives.

Status of Staff

The length of time a person has been in the company confers status to him or her. Foreign companies stress employee competence as a criterion for promotion while Thai companies place more emphasis on the number of years the employee has been in the company. Thais believe that the longer they have been with a company, the more competent they are in protecting the interests of the company. It is important to consider the loyalty of the employee when giving out promotions and awards.

The size of the bonus you give each year is a good way of bestowing status to staff, as is the annual salary increment. Increasing the size of the employee's office, assigning a secretary to the employee or adding to the number of people reporting to him or her are also good ways of conferring status.

A letter of commendation, a certificate of merit or other awards given to good staff will encourage them to work harder. Honours must be given in a way that is public enough that colleagues notice but also circumspectly enough that the recipient does not feel isolated from his colleagues. Public praise is not necessarily a good way of enhancing a staff member's status as it may make other staff envious. When you confer an honour, do not expect gratitude—expect increased productivity and loyalty.

Supervision

Management systems that have been tried and tested at the headquarters back home may not work in the Thai regional office.

Expatriate managers will need to change their management style in Thailand. Do not wait for staff to bring progress reports to you. You should follow up on staff progress to make sure that the staff meet deadlines. This could also be the time to show support for staff rather than making it a mere check-up on their ability to get the job done.

Thai managers make unilateral decisions and they expect the expatriate managers to do the same. This is a double-edged sword: you are expected to be aware of all problems and also take responsibility for bad results.

With initiative and follow-up lying on the manager's shoulders, you may think that the Thai management style is an authoritarian one. This is true, but the style is in a way more paternal than authoritarian. Most of the time, Thai staff look to their managers for guidance and understanding.

Private versus Professional Life
A Thai's private life and professional life often meld together. Thais do not attempt to make any distinction between social relationships and work relationships, and friendships easily cross the line between work and play.

In the West, for example, private life and professional life are normally kept separate. For the Westerner, the formation of familiar relationships with colleagues takes a backseat to results and efficiency at work. In fact, employees within these organisations are generally in competition with one another.

For the Thai, an ideal work environment is one where everyone works in one big group, each with a specified task— with plenty of opportunities for chitchat. Keeping in mind that Thai staff see more of their co-workers than their own family and friends in a given week, having a happy work group makes perfect sense. Thais see their work roles as relationship-oriented rather than task-oriented.

Foreigners generally appreciate the relationships with Thai co-workers and regard this warm working environment as a breath of fresh air.

Dos and Don'ts at the Workplace

You can probably improve productivity and the quality of work by combining some of the already established social customs of your staff and incorporating some of your own incentives. The following is a useful list:

- Do take time to talk to your staff. Do you know your secretary's hometown or your sales manager's favourite sport? A small birthday party is a good way to show interest in staff and gives everyone a chance to socialise. Let your staff know that you care about them and are willing to listen and advice, but that you want a fair day's work in exchange.
- Do work on team-building. Incentives should be aimed at creating and maintaining a consistent and happy team rather than emphasising individual competition and individual rewards. Incentives rewarding individual successes only pitches staff against one another and destroys any team spirit.
- Do allocate work space with regard to your staff's wishes and status. Relationships are affected by the amount of privacy and space you give your staff. Back at headquarters, you may have had your office area partitioned to facilitate good work. Your Thai staff, however, would likely welcome an office with an open concept, which allows them to work with other staff. An exception to the rule is senior staff, who expect private office space to reflect their status—the more senior the staff, the bigger the space.
- Do look for friendship patterns among your staff. Thai staff tend to develop loyalty to a person rather than to an organisation. It is common to hear of whole work teams following a popular department manager who has resigned from an organisation. Such a loss of trained staff can be disastrous in an economy where there are not enough skilled people to fill the growing number of specialised positions. Before you remove a department head, consider who else you will lose if he goes.

- Do plan for future emergencies. Building up goodwill by helping others in the office is sometimes a calculated plan. In this way, there is a very good chance that you can rely on these people later when there is a pressing deadline.
- Do request deadlines; do not order them. Instead of demanding that "100 widgets must be produced in 12 months", you should instead request, "How many widgets do you expect to produce in 12 months?" This puts less pressure on the relationship between you and the staff, and allows staff to update you on developments on the shop floor. When you listen to the staff, they are more likely to respond to your requests.
- Do not distance yourself from your Thai employees. For example, Thais buy snacks to eat in the office but they always buy a little extra so there is enough to share with the other employees. It would be good to occasionally do the same, especially if you eat the snacks they leave in the office pantry.

Social Activities

Provide opportunities for social encounters that supplement work patterns if you can. Seminars, conventions and weekend staff meetings can be beneficial both for work and friendships.

You may be invited to social functions such as a wedding, a funeral or a new year party. Participation in these functions could improve your relationship with your staff. You may find that after participating in one of these events, your staff become more responsive to meeting deadlines and more willing to work late during busy periods.

Thai Weddings You, as the expatriate manager, are very likely to be invited to the wedding of one of your staff members. Sometimes, you may even be asked to make a speech. Do not be surprised to find the wedding set on a weekday—the auspicious date is chosen by a Buddhist monk and may fall on any day or time.

Many Thai weddings are held outdoors, where both the bride and guests exchange gifts. However, most weddings of the middle-class are held indoors. They are usually elaborate and expensive affairs.

You can graciously refuse the invitation when you receive it, but there is an obligation to give a gift of money. Traditionally, the couple moves in with the bride's parents and does not need household items. Money, on the other hand, will help to cover the dowry or "bride price" and the wedding expenses. Remember that your contribution should reflect your seniority within the company. The money should be placed in an envelope marked clearly with your name and company, and given to the bride and groom or to the person at the reception desk at the entrance of the function. If you decide not to attend, give the money to someone else to present on your behalf at the ceremony.

Do not expect to receive thanks from the lucky couple after the wedding. This does not mean that your contribution goes unnoticed. To the Thais, expressing thanks means that the receiver may be asking for more money.

A Thai wedding consists of two ceremonies. The wedding begins in the morning with the blessing ceremony, where monks bless the bride and groom and the wedding guests. This is usually held in the house of the bride's family. You would be required to sit and listen to the monks chant, and then offer food to the monks that would have already been prepared for you. If you are a female, instead of handing food directly to the monk, you should place the plate of food in front of him on a piece of cloth. This practice is in accordance with the monk's vow of celibacy and should not be regarded as sexual discrimination.

Later in the day, there is the water pouring ceremony, where guests gather to pour lustral water over the couple's hands. It is usually held in a larger room such as a hotel function room—a common practice in Bangkok. An informal party ends the day and you may be asked to give a speech—which, incidentally, should be a short one. Try to go to the water pouring ceremony at least if you do not have time for both ceremonies.

Thai Funerals   Thai funerals are usually held within temple grounds, unless the family is not Buddhist. Typically, Thais perform cremations rather than burials, unless the family is of Chinese descent. Women should always wear simple plain black outfits and men should be in dark suits and ties. Avoid bright colours. Pieces of red string are handed out to guests when they arrive to tie onto their wrist or clothing. The red string is believed to protect one against spirits. The casket is raised up on a stand decorated with fresh flowers and wreaths, and a large portrait of the deceased stands next to the casket.

It is appropriate to arrange a flower wreath bearing your condolence message, your name and/or the name of your company to be placed near the casket stand. You may also be asked to participate in gift-giving to the monks at the temple. This will be prearranged by the family of the deceased. Sometime during the evening, plates of food may be offered to funeral guests, usually consisting of rice porridge. If this is not your favourite dish, do not feel obliged to eat it.

A cash contribution is a nice gesture and can be used by the family of the deceased for the funeral expenses. However, this monetary contribution is not seen as a gift but rather as "making merit" or *tum boon*. Check with your Thai friends as to how much you should give, as the amount should reflect your status appropriately. If you decide not to go to the funeral, have an office colleague take your *tum boon* money to present on your behalf.

Before the final cremation ceremony, a series of evening merit-making events are held. People go to the wat for prayers and may be offered a snack to eat. You are expected to make a donation at the wat. Where the deceased is a very senior or close colleague, a Thai company would usually sponsor one of the chanting sessions at the temple and take the lead as host, taking care of most procedures for that evening.

At the cremation ceremony, you are expected to join the other guests in placing a small decorative flower made from wood shavings in the funeral pyre. As each guest exits from the crematorium, they are given a souvenir on a subject that was a favourite of the deceased, such as a book.

New Year   There are three new year celebrations in Thailand. There is the international New Year on 1 January, the Chinese New Year in early February and the Thai Songkran New Year in April, which is marked by a formal holiday. Your staff will expect a party on these occasions, usually consisting of a long lunch party with games, a staff gift exchange and music. Several of your most sociable staff will be busy making arrangements for these parties days beforehand.

There will be gift-giving and, once again, the value of the gift is determined by the role and status of the giver and the recipient, as well as the nature of the relationship. It is the practice to distribute presents to those who work directly under you. The rule of thumb is to keep the gift simple.

If you are managing a large enterprise, you need not give presents to everybody. As an alternative, sponsor the office party to show your appreciation of all staff. Try to include a speech and if you can manage it, include a raffle with unwrapped bottles of whiskey, quality coffee or other functional items as prizes. New Year's day can also be a time to reward outstanding staff.

You may also use this time to present gifts to outstanding customers or to people of social prominence that have been helpful to your business like company directors, well-connected friends and government officials. Ask your staff for advice in this area.

Employing Staff

The Thai way is to maintain good relationships not only at the workplace but also with friends and relatives outside the office. In village culture, your family and neighbours are important and you should help them in difficult times, for example, when they are unemployed. Therefore, expatriate managers must be aware of the possible negative effects of your staff favouring family members over strangers when it comes to staff recruitment, selection of contract tenders and promotions. However, you can allow for favouritism where it would help your office working community.

For example, your accounts manager might select a relative as his assistant over better qualified applicants because he is sure that he is getting someone he can trust—after all, his relative has an obligation to family that other applicants cannot offer. However, if the relative is lazy and you know your manager is supporting his relative's application because he is obliged to, remember that you have the final say.

Women in Thailand

In Thailand, women are admired for their beauty and valued for their childbearing ability. However, women are under-represented in government and subject to a double standard. The status of women in Thailand is almost exactly what it was in the West before the turn of the century.

The clear-cut separation of male and female roles are taught to children from a young age. Children see their father as the more powerful figure in the household with more contact with the public domain, while their mother is seen as being primarily responsible for the family's well-being. There is a Thai saying that the wife is the hind legs of the elephant while the husband is the front legs.

Women who do not observe proper dress and behavioural codes will be the subject of workplace gossip. On the other hand, Thais accept men's infidelity as normal, and Thai men seem to be proud of their ability to support one or more girlfriends and/or wives. Keeping a "major" and a "minor" wife (*meea noi*) was widely practised in the past and is still common today. Even the highly-respected King Chulalongkorn had numerous wives and children.

Throughout the six decades of democracy, female Ministers of Parliament have never accounted for more than 7% of the House. Today, many universities use a quota system that favours male students in subjects such as veterinary science, marine science and archaeology.

The difference between the treatment of men and women in the workforce starts at the recruitment stage. A typical example of recruitment advertisements in Thailand: "Manager wanted, 30 to 35 years of age, Thai national, *male only*". Equally disconcerting is the advertisement for *"pretty Thai girls* between 20 and 25" for front desk and so-called PR jobs. Equal opportunity is a concept that most Thai companies have yet to grasp or apply.

Providing a suitable heir—especially since large families are actively discouraged in Thailand—is very important to the Thai woman. Yet if she has a baby, she may lose her job, even though laws protect her right to maternity leave.

Women are also expected to retire earlier than men. Before 1996, female crew members employed in Thai Airways International had to retire at 45—compared to 60 years for male crew—and were prohibited from having more than two children or having a baby during the first four years of work. Furthermore, their salary was cut during their pregnancy.

As a male expatriate manager, you may be invited by a male colleague to go *teeo puying* or visit a massage parlour. Although it is perfectly acceptable to visit the women in a massage parlour, you should on no account give your secretary so much as a friendly pat on the back for a job well done. This could ruin her standing with the other staff and you could end up with a reputation for manhandling female staff .

If you are changing a work roster for your staff, bear in mind the propriety of putting men and women on the same job if such an arrangement could cause unwelcome gossip.

Some women do reach positions of power in Thailand by owning and operating hotels, schools, stores and industries. To reach a high status in the Thai business world, a woman must have either very good social connections, great wealth, a formidable intellect, relentless perseverance, or a combination of all four. Such a woman can be a powerful ally or an implacable enemy.

Confrontation versus Conflict Avoidance

The Western way of thinking is that confrontation can be good if it means that it results in better understanding or a better way to get a job done. It is acceptable for two people to be critical of each other's ideas or methods, then shake hands and go off to enjoy a beer together after work, whether or not an agreement was reached. In the West, such an activity is not seen as an argument but a debate.

Constructive criticism is not a Thai concept. Few Thais can tolerate raised voices and expressions of frustration or anger. What expatriates see as evidence of hard work and constructive criticism, the Thais see as disrespect, demotivation and pushiness.

Thais expect you to try to do everything, even when infuriated, without shouting. Being nice when things go wrong gives the wrongdoer the chance to realise his or her mistake and make amends. This in turn builds a long-term obligation to provide service or to do the job properly or more quickly the next time. Even being "too serious" can be seen as a poor character trait—anyone who is serious all the time will be seen as being altogether too demanding.

At the same time, displays of dismay, despair, enthusiasm or disapproval are frowned upon. Accordingly, the person who is or appears to be serenely indifferent (*choei choei*) is respected for having what is considered an important virtue. When something unfortunate or unplanned happens, you will often hear the words *"mai pen rai"* which translates roughly to "don't worry about it" or "it doesn't matter". These words are used to keep people on a path between extremes so as to avoid any feelings of conflict—the Buddhist "middle path".

Thais try to find a way of reaching goals that keeps relationships intact and this can be overly compromising. Though everyone may be happy, no work may be accomplished because the plan is too vague.

Office Conflicts

There will eventually come a time when you have to point out to someone that they are doing something wrong. If you have to criticise somebody, do it away from the public eye so that your staff can "save face". A Thai criticised in public will give little thought as to whether your criticism is fair or unfair, and will go to great lengths to avoid you in the future.

Bring the person you want to talk to into your office. Being called to the boss's office is already a warning to Thai staff that something is wrong. In the West, an employee is usually disciplined as soon as the mistake is discovered. However, in Thailand, try to pick a time when you are calm and are in full control of yourself and the situation. Try to keep things pleasant by balancing criticism with praise rather than continually reprimanding staff. Offering the staff "what if" suggestions is a good way to camouflage criticism. If you suspect somebody has not fully understood you, do not raise your voice. Repeat yourself calmly but do not shout.

Explaining that it is you and not the staff who will be held responsible for a mistake by the head office can motivate staff to correct their ways and help keep you out of trouble. Whether or not they will do this depends on how much you have worked on your relationship with them and how much they like you. In the same vein, when one of your staff reports the wrongdoing of another staff, do not display your anger openly. The staff reporting may wrongly interpret that your anger is directed at them rather than at the staff who has erred.

If there is conflict between two staff members and you are asked to solve the problem, it is better to see each person individually. The best solution might be to separate the two so that they do not come into daily contact. If, on the other hand, their work depends upon interaction, you might have no choice but to spend some time with the staff members and point out the importance of working together. Sideways promotion is also a very good way of moving someone who is in trouble out of the line of fire. In government, this ploy is called "being transferred to an inactive post".

Frank and Direct versus Kreng Jai

Closely related to conflict avoidance is the Thai value of *kreng jai*. In your office back home, getting to the facts and dealing with them directly, openly and honestly is important for good working relations. Frankness is valued and "getting to the point" is popular with managers. People who speak their minds clearly and plainly are valued.

The Thai word *kreng jai* is hard to translate and explain in English, because such a concept does not exist in the Western world. *Kreng jai* is used by the Thais to keep a relationship pleasant and cooperative, and accounts for a lot of the politeness and civility found in Thai society. *Kreng jai* results in your Thai staff's reluctance to disturb you with an important telephone message when you are in a meeting with a colleague, to ask for a lift from you to the post office even though they know you pass it every day and the unwillingness to ask questions in meetings so as not to disturb you or the flow of the meeting. If you, as a boss, are fairly intense and driven, you can almost be guaranteed that your staff will keep away and not "disturb" you with their work.

If you are a senior manager, *kreng jai* will guarantee that if you make unintentional mistakes, your staff will not tell you about it or, at best, will try to cover up your wrongdoing. Be aware of this fact, as it prevents you from blaming staff for the mistakes you committed six months earlier.

Thais are generally not very assertive in the office for a number of reasons. It may be a simple matter of *kreng jai* or it could be a result of their education. Thai students rarely question their teachers as it is seen as attention-seeking behaviour at best and questioning the wisdom of the teacher at worst. Such a trait may have arisen from an exaggerated respect for the boss (or fear of losing a job) or simply a matter of difficulty with English.

As an expatriate, you can reduce the stress of your staff by slowing down your speech and listening extra carefully. Give your staff time to find the right words in English and listen to what is being implied through their body language as well. By keeping your door open, you are already inviting anyone who walks past your office to stop and talk. When they do drop in, listen.

You should respect the fact that by being *kreng jai*, your Thai staff is trying to be polite to you and your position. Continued efforts to show your patience and receptiveness to employee's questions, opinions and objections will reduce your staff's use of *kreng jai* over time.

Summary

In a country where an ordered hierarchy was the norm until recently and old ways still exist, you and your staff will need to negotiate each situation as it occurs.

You cannot change a culture but you can influence culture at the workplace. By adapting ingrained Thai attitudes to authority and ritual, you will gain a new understanding of the Thai way of working and the relationships possible at work.

The Thai way can be infuriating at times but it can be fun too. It can make your job a misery or a pleasure. Your business experience will be totally coloured by what you do to accommodate and adapt to the Thai way.

CHAPTER 8

Communicating at Work

Effective communication is based on speaking clearly and listening carefully to what the other party is saying. Initially, you may have problems understanding what your Thai counterparts are trying to communicate to you via their words and body language. However, if you are aware of the problems involved, you will be able to implement your plans with a minimum of difficulty.

Thai Time

Thais use the Buddhist calendar and a unique method of dividing the number of hours in each day. Unless you get used to this, referring to the concept of time in your conversations with Thais can be rather confusing!

The Buddhist Year

The Thais follow the Buddhist year and their calendar is set 243 years ahead of the Gregorian calendar that Westerners are used to. For example, the year 1998 as understood by Westerners usually appears in government and legal documents and Thai calendars as 2541. Fortunately, the number of months and days per month in the Buddhist calendar is similar to that of the Gregorian one, so Thais celebrate New Year's day on the same day as Westerners.

Thai staff usually think of years in terms of the Buddhist calendar. To avoid confusion, always talk in terms of "in 10 years time" or "five years ago" rather than naming specific years. This will allow the listener to make a mental reference according to his or her own calendar rather than having to shift from one calendar to another.

Daily Time

In Western countries, there tends to be a distinction between time reserved for work and time meant for relaxation. Business people in the West are particularly conscious of the value of time and meeting deadlines.

Thais, on the other hand, are not ruled by the clock. Fully enjoying one's time and interacting with others is more important than meeting deadlines. Things are only dealt with as they come up, which often means things get done in a flurry of activity at the last minute.

Given Thailand's rural background and belief in Buddhism, it is not difficult to understand the apparent indifference to immediate earthly goals. However note that Thais do set goals. They simply appear to be more accepting of the way things work out.

Thai Time

In Western culture, the 24-hour day is broadly divided into day and night. In Thailand, the day is divided into seven segments. These are:

• Early morning	1 a.m. to 6.59 a.m.
• Late morning	7 a.m. to 11.59 a.m.
• Noon	12 p.m. to 12.59 p.m.
• Early afternoon	1 p.m. to 3.59 p.m.
• Late afternoon	4 p.m. to 6.59 p.m.
• Evening	7 p.m. to 11.59 p.m.
• Midnight	12 a.m. to 12.59 a.m.

Communication problems are obvious when you realise, for example, that there are two mornings according to the Thai clock. When a Thai says 2 o'clock in the morning, he may well mean 8 a.m., which is the second hour of the late morning. Similarly, a Thai who says 3 o'clock in the evening often means the third hour of the evening segment or 9 p.m. Most of the time, communication problems have to do with the two morning and one evening segments. The best way to get around this problem is to actually point to the hour on the watch face or use military time—that is, say 1300 hours when you mean 1 p.m.

Punctuality and Reliability

In keeping their appointments, Thais desire a certain amount of flexibility. If a Thai arranges to meet you at your office at 10 o'clock, expect him or her to arrive somewhere between 10 and 11. Do not expect a telephone call to say that he or she is running late. The likelihood of being on time is made less so by the traffic situation in Bangkok. Thais often blame the traffic for their being late, even if this is not really the case. Thais also sometimes cancel appointments at the last minute, so do not be offended. Have a contingency plan and work schedule just in case.

The Thai view of time is shaped by their general outlook of acceptance. This is not to say that Thais approve of an uncomfortable situation, such as a traffic jam. They feel that the government should do something to correct the situation, but at present, they accept that it is difficult to solve. This calm acceptance of a trying situation may seem extreme to an expatriate.

In Thailand there is more focus on "being" rather than "doing". Thais will regard a mountain peak as something to admire while Westerners are often more likely to regard it as something to climb.

Ironically, you, as a foreigner, are expected to be punctual and reliable, and comments will be made if you are late or change an appointment. Whether you want to provide an example to your staff in matters of punctuality and reliability is your choice.

Thai Values

The following are values that Thais admire in a good manager. They are worth mentioning because they motivate staff. For example, showing concern for your Thai staff would make you seem an inspiring manager.

Respect for Authority or Hai Khiad

The act of *hai khiad* demonstrates respect or honour for someone. *Hai khiad* runs two ways between a superior and junior. When a boss attends the wedding or funeral ceremony of an employee, and if he takes the time to greet his staff by name and chats or asks advice from his employees, he is expressing *hai khiad* to his staff. This creates feelings of indebtedness in the employee that will one day be returned. Showing *hai khiad* to junior staff is more at the boss's discretion than the junior's.

When junior and senior staff *wai*, the junior always *wais* first as a sign of *hai khiad*. A junior will also *wai* a senior to express thanks when receiving a salary cheque, for example.

Kindness or Nam Jai

The word *nam* means water while *jai* means heart. Put the two words together and you have "water from the heart". This phrase has a meaning similar to the English saying "milk of human kindness". *Nam jai* means to extend kindness to others without the expectation of anything in return.

Thais admire a manager who, after going on a trip abroad, returns with small gifts for everyone. Or one who returns from lunch with snacks for the staff. A stranger on the street is extending *nam jai* to you if he or she patiently explains to you how to get to your destination.

Sympathy or Hen Jai

To *hen jai* or to "see heart" refers to the ability to understand or empathise with people. When you accommodate an employee whose wife has just had a baby and needs time off work, you have demonstrated the quality of *hen jai*. Similarly, if you take the time to listen to your staff and see how heavy their workload is before assigning them another task, you are showing *hen jai*.

Calmness or Sam Ruam

This value is derived from the Buddhist concept of the "middle path". Thais believe that one should exercise restraint in situations, which, in the West, would usually lead to displays of extreme emotions of anger, happiness, frustration or sadness. For example, Thais express anger with a subdued look rather than shouting and banging their fists on tables. Similarly, if a Thai is frustrated that the fax line is out of service, he or she will keep his emotions to himself. If a friend or relative has died, you should not show grief openly as this will make others feel uncomfortable.

The more senior you are, the more you are expected to show self-control. This trait is roughly equivalent to the British desire to keep a "stiff upper lip".

Communication

Not all differences between foreigners and Thais are related to clashes in values. Certain differences between foreigners and Thais pertain to the way they communicate in writing and speaking.

Thais do not expect a foreigner to master the language or know all the rules when interacting with them during their few years in Thailand. However, it is important that a foreigner at least tries to understand the conventions of Thai communication.

Written Thai

The Thai alphabet is based on Sanskrit and contains 46 consonants, of which two are obsolete. There are also 36 vowel symbols or symbol clusters, which are divided into long and short forms.

If you plan to stay in Thailand for some time and do not want to use a translator for your documents, it will be necessary to learn to read and write Thai.

Spoken Thai

Pronunciation of the Thai language is entirely regular. You might think 36 vowels is a bit excessive, but Thais would argue that the five vowels in the English language are entirely inadequate when considering that there are more than 30 vowel sounds in the language. In contrast, each vowel sound in Thai has a unique symbol to identify it. The language is pronounced exactly the way it is written and contains a minimum of irregularities.

The Thai language has simple grammar rules. Object follows subject. There are no genders, plurals or articles, almost no tenses, and very few prepositions. Vocabulary is formed by combinations of simpler words—a little like German. For example the word for "sock" is a combination of the word for "foot" and the word for "bag". The word *"samlor"*—the three wheeled mini-taxis very popular in Thailand—is made up of the word *"sam"* for "three" and *"lor"* for "wheel". There are thousands of other examples.

For the English speaker, the most difficult aspect of learning Thai is mastering and pronouncing the five tones—middle, low, falling, high and rising. Unless you use the tones correctly, many Thais will not understand what you are saying. In fact, they may not even recognise that you are trying to speak Thai!

Politeness in Speaking Thai

If French is known as the language of love and Italian the language of fine music, then Thai is the language of politeness. Thai has dozens of words that show respect, with different words used for differences in age and hierarchy between two people. For example, while the pronouns "I" and "You" can be used by just about every speaker of the English language, in Thai, the usage of these pronouns change depending on whether you are speaking to a close friend, your spouse, a five-year old child, a teacher, your aunt or your parents. And then, if you are talking about royalty, Buddhist monks or the Lord Buddha, you should use a form of higher Thai.

Not to have an array of pronouns to show respect for differences in age and hierarchy can be a real problem for the Thais. For example, when Thais are forced to speak English amongst themselves, they are denied the ability to show adequate respect for one another. A group of Thais—even if a foreigner is present— will often slip into their own language to avoid the problem of not showing respect to a senior person.

Apart from using pronouns to show respect, the Thai language has words that are added to the end of a sentence but have no real meaning at all. They are only used to demonstrate politeness. Females add the word *khaa* at the end of their sentences and males add the word *khrup*. When a Thai is communicating an instruction, the listener will usually use the word *khrup* or *khaa* to acknowledge what the speaker has spoken. However, *khrup* and *khaa* do not actually mean "Yes, I understand" unless it is said with the right intensity. Sometimes, you will think that your listener agrees with you when all he has said is "I hear you".

If you decide to learn to speak Thai, be sure to learn from someone who knows the different levels of politeness and is not afraid to tell you when you are too polite to the driver or too casual with your colleagues.

Names, Titles and Introductions
Apart from pronouns, Thais also use names and titles to reflect status and relationships among people—as elaborated below.

Full Names, Nicknames and Khun Thais have a first name and a surname—the family name—following the first name. Thais have no middle names. The use of the first name and family name is usually reserved for formal matters.

Nearly all Thais have nicknames, which are used among family and friends, and in an office where staff feel comfortable with one another. However, managers in higher positions will not allow others to call them by their nicknames. The advantage of nicknames is that they are easier to remember as they have far fewer syllables than formal names and usually have a meaning attached to them.

You would be surprised at the mix of Thai words used as nicknames—pig, fertiliser, chicken, shorty, gemstone and so on. Such nicknames are not considered derogatory nor are they demeaning to one's physical appearance or character. Thais see pigs as cuddly and adorable animals, thus the popularity of this nickname. No one has the nickname "dog", as most Thais consider dogs to be unclean animals—you need only look at the stray dogs in Bangkok to understand this. This is quite the opposite of the Western view of a dog being a man's best friend and "pig" being a word used to curse others.

When you are introduced to someone for the first time, the atmosphere is more formal. Here, first names are used, regardless of the status of the other party. In Thailand, first names are always formal. This is in contrast to the West where the use of first names is usually reserved for informal situations to convey friendliness and familiarity.

To convey politeness, the Thai language has a series of prefixes to use before a person's name. Thais use them with a person's name even when they are speaking English. All of them are used in the second or third person. *Khun* is the most common prefix. *Khun* can be used with a person's first name or nickname. It translates roughly to the English equivalents of Mr, Mrs and Miss. *Khun* is a handy word because you can sometimes use it by itself to refer to people you are talking to if you do not know their names.

A woman, either single or married, is addressed by her first name with the word *Khun* as a prefix. As in many other countries, women take on their husbands' surnames.

The More Formal Nai and Tun   There are other ways of addressing people to indicate their higher status. These prefixes are used only with a person's formal first name.

Nai is a prefix used with a man's name and Thai staff would most likely add *Nai* in front of the name of any male who is in top-level management. In these cases, *Nai* then takes the place of *Khun*. However, as the word *Nai* does not "mesh well" with Western names, Thai staff often adopt the foreign titles of Mr, Miss, Sir and Doctor when addressing foreigners in top-level management. So in the office, you may be referred to as Mr John, Mrs Jane and so on.

Tun is a prefix used for either a male or female of high rank such as important government servants and dignitaries. It shows respect for someone's rank rather than a personal respect. Like the prefix *Nai*, it is never used as a prefix for a person's name if he or she is of a lower rank. Many of the top ranking government officials use this title.

Titles in Thai Society Important people connected with royalty, the civil service and the military have titles that are used in place of *Khun*, *Nai* or *Than*.

If a Thai holds or has held an important position such as that of a university lecturer, he or she may use the word *Ahjarn*, meaning "teacher", in front of his or her first name. This also applies for those who are in the military or have retired from it. These people expect others to address them by their title, even if they have retired or have not lectured in years.

There is a title that is given specifically to women in Thailand. Each year, the king bestows the title of *Khunying* or the higher title of *Tanpuying* on women who have contributed to the development of the country or whose support has been crucial to the success of their husbands. These titles are used in place of *Khun* or *Tun*. Most of the women who have been honoured come from the highest business and government positions. You will often see the names and faces of various *Khunyings* and *Tanpuyings* in the high society pages of the Thai daily newspapers.

> **Royal Titles**
> Royal titles last only till the fifth generation, then they are no longer used. Any title should be displayed in abbreviated form on letters and invitations. The title holder would most likely use it on his or her business card. The titles appear in descending order of importance, as follows:
>
> - P.O.C.: *Phra Ong Chao*, grandchild of king
> - M.C.: *Mom Chao*, child of P.O.C
> - M.R.: *Mom Rajawong*, child of M.C.
> - M.L.: *Mom Luang*, child or wife of M.R. and wife of M.C.
>
> Important civil service titles, presented in descending order, are as follows:
>
> - *Chao Phya* (The *Chao Phya's* wife is *Khun Ying*)
> - *Phya*
> - *Phra*
> - *Luang*
> - *Khun* (In Thai, it is spelt and pronounced differently from the *Khun* meaning 'you' or 'Mr')
>
> Source: *Thais Mean Business*, Robert Cooper

The English Language

Spoken English

Spoken English is a real challenge to many Thais partly because they learned the basics of English from Thai teachers during their high school years. Thai government schools rarely have sound laboratories and often have very large classes (50 or more students). Thai teachers concentrate on reading and writing and often have little training in spoken English themselves. A Thai high school graduate may therefore be familiar with an English word only when it is pronounced with a Thai accent. As a result of Thais' limited

---

English: The Universal Language
One of the authors recently attended a conference between Japanese and Thai business people, where negotiations were conducted entirely in the halting English of both parties—their common language. The subsequent agreement was written in English and signed with the English signatures of the two contracting parties.

More and more English language documentation is used in Thailand—even between Thais.

English education and the inadequate English vocabulary for the acknowledgement of status and respect, speaking in English is hard work for them.

When staff hear an instruction, they will normally check with a colleague as to the right meaning rather than ask questions to check understanding. The staff are not only too *kreng jai* to bother the boss with questions, but also do not want to appear ignorant. Remember that Thais have been taught to follow instructions from their parents and teachers, rather than question or express opinions and assert what they feel is right.

So what must a foreigner do to allow Thais to cope?

You should speak slowly and simplify your sentences. Use the present tense if possible, as the Thai language does not have irregular verbs. Listeners may not recognise the connection between "went" and "to go", and "was" and "to be". Remember also that your staff are unlikely to be familiar with slang words.

Do not raise your voice if your Thai staff do not understand you. Thais are sensitive to a raised voice and associate it with conflict. You should slow down and pronounce your words clearly.

Thais have a habit of answering "Yes" to any question whether they understand it or not—like the Thai words *khrup* and *khao*. The tendency of Thai subordinates to do this is magnified the higher the manager is in the company hierarchy because of the higher amount of *kreng jai* involved. If you pose a question and you are not sure if the answer "Yes" actually means understanding, look at body language for clues—a nervous stance, a worried look, a hesitant answer. Otherwise, try to ask open-ended questions such as "How much photocopy paper is left?" rather than yes-and-no questions such as "Is there any photocopy paper left?"

To check understanding, you can always ask for your instructions to be repeated, although your staff might think that you do not have full confidence in them. If you do rely on the repetition of instructions, emphasise to the listener that you distrust your own ability to give instructions rather than the fact that you doubt the employee's ability to understand.

Always follow up your instructions by casually meeting with staff to see how work is progressing. If the project is going well, use this opportunity to praise them. You can be sure that your Thai staff will respond positively. If things are going wrong, rather than giving criticism, give "what if" suggestions that would make things work better. Always do this discreetly so that your staff "save face" in front of co-workers.

Generally, problems will become less frequent as you get used to the Thai ways of speaking English and your staff get used to your way of speaking English. A routine where certain word patterns go along with specific actions will evolve.

Foreigners are often surprised at Thai bluntness. Some comments and questions seem out of the Thai character of *kreng jai*, or not wanting to make others feel uncomfortable. Sample phrases are listed below.

- "Hi John. I see that you are looking very fat today. You must be very rich."
- Oh, Mary, you've been stuck in traffic all morning. Would you like to use the bathroom? You must be wanting to urinate."
- "I heard that you have a new job in an American company. Foreign

companies pay quite well you know. How much is your salary?"

- "Where are you going? Have you eaten yet?"

In Thailand, such questions are quite acceptable and comments like these are usually from Thais who think in Thai but speak in English. Such comments on one's physical appearance or eating habits can be explained by Thailand's agricultural culture. If you are looking thin, Thais will comment on it to show interest in your well-being. It should not be taken as a criticism that you are not taking care of yourself.

Privacy is not highly-valued in Thailand so office chitchat amongst staff is likely to be about one's personal life and feelings rather than about the weather and sports. Such questions also serve to give some context as to where you stand in the social hierarchy. For example, questions about salary would indicate (to the person asking) other people's positions in the company hierarchy.

Keep in mind that Thais mean no harm with such comments and questions, and do not realise that such remarks can be interpreted by foreigners as rude or overly direct. If a Thai makes such a comment it is best just to nod your head or smile. Do not take offence at such comments.

Written Communication

It is better to give your staff a memo stating exactly what you want done, then meet with them to have them discuss the instructions with you. Thais are more skilled at reading English than writing, listening to or speaking the language. If your staff fail to follow verbal instructions or what was said in meetings, you can usually get the message across in writing. With a dictionary and help from other staff, even the weakest English speaker can interpret what is written.

However, Thais are often reluctant to write because they fear that they may express themselves poorly and that their peers will see their poor writing. They also fear writing because the written word is associated with authority and power in Thailand and staff may feel that what they write will be "set in concrete"—that is, too final and definite.

Do not impose expectations on your staff that all their written correspondences have to be perfect. As long as your staff are getting the message across and the correspondence is not going to a major buyer or the head office, turn a blind eye to minor errors. Correcting English takes time and if you do it too often, your staff will become reluctant to submit written communication to you so as to "save face".

Even if the person you are sending correspondence to is a Thai who speaks good English—many Thai business people are educated abroad today—it is still a good idea to send the original letter in Thai with an English translation attached to it. This will show appreciation of the fact that the receiver may not open and read all letters himself, or that he may want to circulate your letter within his organisation before answering.

The recipient will be assured that he can answer in Thai, which is often desirable because Thais who write in English often leave unclear messages unintentionally. It is embarrassing to both sides to have to seek clarifications. Translation then becomes the responsibility of your office, not the staff's, and it is easier for you to seek clarification.

Another advantage of providing bilingual letters is the fact that your English-speaking contact might one day be replaced by one who does not possess such language skills. In this case, the Thai version of your previous correspondences with his or her predecessor will become very useful.

Office Meetings

In many countries, meetings are democratic affairs where everyone is expected to contribute. In these places, meetings are seen as problem-solving situations rather than occasions where management hands down company directives. Everyone is expected to contribute his or her expertise during brainstorming sessions. You need not wait to be asked to give an opinion or to question the opinion of others. If you give an opinion that is wrong, you are at least given credit for participating and attempting to be accountable for your responsibilities.

In Thailand, however, meetings are always formal affairs where the staff sit and listen to company directives issued by upper management. There is no contribution of ideas by staff, unless they are invited to do so by management—in which case, input is respectfully discreet. The duty of the staff is to sit, listen and take notes on those matters that concern them. Questions are hardly asked because of the fear that the question would be seen as a criticism of the chairperson.

Thais' passiveness in meetings also arises from the language barrier. To successfully participate in a meeting conducted by a foreigner, you must have the verbal skills to present your thoughts and defend your position. You also need to be confident and assertive. Given the linguistic and cultural differences between Thais and Westerners, native English speakers tend to dominate meetings.

If you are going to chair a meeting, circulate a written agenda outlining topics to be covered during the meeting. These topics should be ideas offered by staff during private consultations. Before the meeting, check to see what people's opinions and ideas are, and ask the staff to express these ideas during the meeting. Applaud any contribution your staff make to the meeting. If you cannot get anyone to participate during a meeting, to get staff input, you may need to rely on the open-door policy, where you get to talk to each staff personally in your office.

Remember that the more people you invite to a meeting, the greater the chances of hierarchy barriers among staff, so keep numbers low. Be aware that Thais are sometimes reluctant to speak out, particularly in English, because they fear that their peers will perceive them as trying to stand out. Encourage staff to listen to one another and give non-native English speakers time to compose their ideas.

To encourage Thai staff's input, allowing them to occasionally discuss a point in Thai and then translate it for you. If someone offers an idea that is obviously wrong, avoid saying a blunt "No". Try self-correction and peer-correction techniques, with expressions such as "Anybody else?"

When the meeting is long, you will notice staff chatting quietly in groups of twos or threes. Thai people talk through funerals, weddings, presentations—and meetings. Do not take offence. Your staff assume that you will repeat yourself. They are only taking the opportunity to socialise with one another.

Body Language

The Body Hierarchy

Thais believe in a body hierarchy. The head is seen as the seat of one's "living essence" or soul and is treated with the greatest respect. The feet are seen as the lowliest and dirtiest part of the body.

Touching another person's head is taboo unless absolutely necessary. Therefore, if your luggage is in the train ceiling rack above another passenger, it is always appropriate to excuse yourself before reaching for your bag. It is acceptable to touch children aged ten and below on the head as a sign of affection. It is also fine for children to touch their close friends on the head. The same goes for those in an intimate relationship.

In Thai language, there is slang word referring to feet, which is considered very impolite to use. The foot is not the proper appendage to use for pointing. Avoid using the foot to point out to your mechanic a wheel on your car or to point out to one of your staff a ream of photocopy paper on the lowest shelf in the stock room. Such behaviour would be seen as an act of superiority that says to the Thai, "You are not important enough to make it necessary for me to use my hand to point with." Feet should not be used to open doors. Neither should they be placed on top of your desk.

Shoe Error
A foreign manager at an exhibition in Bangkok took off her shoe to use as a hammer in an attempt to attach a Thai flag to an exhibition board. The Thai staff were shocked to see their manager waving a shoe around, then bringing it down on the Thai national symbol!

In polite company, Thais avoid crossing their legs because it tends to make the sole of the shoe visible to everyone. In business, it is generally acceptable to sit cross-legged, unless you are, say, an honorary guest at a function and are sitting high on a stage in front of an audience.

When walking past someone much older or more superior than you, lower your body as you walk to show respect. It shows respect for the speaker and politeness to the audience when you try not to obstruct their view. If you are in a crowded hallway and your only way out is to walk between two of your superiors, lower your body as you walk through.

When polite Thais speak, they tend to use a minimum of physical gestures. Lots of gestures only confuse people. Putting your arm around someone or slapping them on the back for a job well done are not Thai habits. Point only to objects, but not sacred objects such as images of Buddha. If you have to distinguish someone from a group, the polite way to do it is to point with your palm facing upwards and your fingers brought together in a pointing fashion. If you need to call someone such as a waitress, do not clap or wave your arms about. Instead, wave your hand towards yourself, palm facing downwards, in a polite fashion.

If you need to pass something to someone, do not throw it no matter how small or insignificant the object may be. Always pass the object by hand, particularly the right hand, if you want to be extra polite. You will notice that Thais support the right hand with the left when they are passing an object to a superior.

This body language not only applies to how you interact with people, but in some cases, how you handle objects. For example, many Thais wear a Buddhist amulet or the picture of one of the royal family an a pendant. If a Thai offers you an amulet as a gift, always put it in your shirt or blouse pocket, never in your trouser or skirt pocket.

Thai Greeting—the Wai

A well-known Thai greeting, the *wai* is not only a way of saying hello and goodbye but is also a way of showing thanks or respect to people and sacred objects like Buddhist statues and spirit houses.

The *wai* is made by raising both hands, palms joined and fingers held upwards, to a position close to the body somewhere between the chest and chin. The elbows are kept close to the body as the hands are raised. The lower the head comes down to meet the hands, the more is the respect shown. The hands move in a slow and graceful manner as they are raised to *wai* then lowered again. There is no difference between showing the *wai* to a male or female.

The *wai* has a lot to do with status and hierarchy. For example, when Thais meet, a person who is junior in age or social rank will always *wai* first. The senior usually *wais* in return by raising the hands only to chest level or merely nodding his head and smiling to acknowledge the greeting. The greater the difference in hierarchy between two people, the less likely the superior will return the *wai*. At the top of the social hierarchy, Buddhist monks never return a *wai* from anyone, not even royalty. In turn, the royal family never *wais* members of the public.

A foreigner may be confused when faced with a choice of shaking hands or using the *wai* to greet someone. As a rule, do not return a *wai* from those lower in the social hierarchy, even if the young child doing the *wai* is extremely adorable or if you think the guard who *wais* you at the gate when you arrive at the factory deserves one in return.

To return such a *wai* would confuse people and make you look silly. Just acknowledge the *wai* with a smile and a nod of the head. Office staff will generally *wai* you to say thank you when receiving their pay. They will also do so when entering or leaving your office, or when requesting your attention when you have guests. Again, a smile and a nod are enough to acknowledge such *wais*.

The people you should always *wai* are monks or Buddha images, members of the royal family and elders—unless the elder is your servant or a street vendor. It is always good to *wai* your important business clients or government contacts at the start of the meeting and before you leave. If someone *wais* you when you have your hands full with a mobile phone or briefcase, it is not necessary to put everything down before returning the *wai*—just lift your hands into the closest *wai* position you can without dropping everything. Otherwise, if you are holding a newspaper, for example, tuck the newspaper under your arm, then *wai*.

As mentioned earlier, the feet is the lowest in the body hierarchy. Therefore, it is impolite to *wai* with a pair of shoes in your hands. It might seem unlikely that such a situation could occur. However, it recently happened to a foreigner who was visiting a Thai colleague at his home. He had just taken his shoes off when his colleague's mother came out to greet him. Shoes in hand, he gave what he thought was a deeply respectful *wai*. Little did he know that, instead of showing respect, he was actually insulting his colleague's mother.

As for shaking hands, if you are male, it is best to stick to shaking hands with other men and giving a combination of a polite smile, a verbal hello and nod to women. If you are a female, it is best to nod, say hello and smile to everyone. Feel comfortable to shake hands with any Thai who offers their hand, regardless of what gender they are.

If you think you have mastered the art of *waiing* but are with a group of foreigners who do not know how to *wai*, it may be better to offer a handshake or nod so as not to make your foreign friends feel out of place. If they see you *wai*, they might think it necessary to do so, which might turn into a comedy of *wai* errors.

Touching

As already discussed, it is best to avoid shaking hands unless your Thai colleague offers his hand first. However, rules on touching go beyond the handshake.

Touching someone of the opposite sex in public is considered inappropriate in Thailand. If you are a male and you think that one of your female staff has done a great job, do not express your approval by patting her on the back. Thais have a habit of reading into such things.

An exception to the rule occurs when you want to get the attention of a friend or a familiar colleague but cannot do so verbally. Here, you can tap them on the elbow.

Touching people of the same sex is fine. Do not be surprised if a colleague of the same sex takes your hand while talking to you. Putting your hands in your pockets will not do any good because your colleague will probably just clasp your forearm instead. If you are talking while sitting at a table, they may place their hand on your knee. In Thailand, this is a sign of friendship and nothing more. Do not pull your hand or leg away, as this would be seen as a refusal of his friendship. The only alternatives are to let your hand go limp until the person lets go of your hand or to just keep your leg still and not pay too much attention to it.

The Smile

One of the first things that we hear about Thailand is that it is "The Land of Smiles". Tourists and first-time visitors remark how often Thais smile. But after being in Thailand for some time, you begin to ask yourself why it is that Thais smile so much, even in situations where a smile would seem out-of-place or rude.

For foreigners, smiling is a show of pleasure. In the Webster's Dictionary, the word "smile" is defined as "a facial expression showing usually pleasure, amusement, affection, friendliness, etc."

But for the Thais, smiling is a general facial expression used to express many different emotions. It is not confined to happiness and pleasure alone. Thais even smile when they have done something terribly wrong and want to make amends.

The Thai Smile

In their book, *Working with the Thais*, Henry Holmes and Suchanda Tangtongtavy give a comprehensive list of Thai smiles. They are:

- *Yim thang nam taa*   The I'm-so-happy-I'm-crying smile
- *Yim thak thaai*   The polite smile for someone you barely know
- *Yim cheun chom*   The I-admire-you smile
- *Fuen yim*   The stiff smile, also known as the I-should-laugh-at-the-joke-though-it's-not-funny smile
- *Yim mee lessanai*   The smile which masks something wicked in mind
- *Yim yaw*   The teasing, or I-told-you-so smile
- *Yim yae-yae*   The I-know-things-look-pretty-bad-but-there's-no-point-in-crying-over-spilt-milk smile
- *Yim sao*   The sad smile
- *Yim haeng*   The dry smile, also known as the I-know-I-owe-you-the-money-but-I-don't-have-it smile
- *Yim thak thaan*   The I-disagree-with-you smile, also known as the You-can-go-ahead-and-propose-it-but-your-idea's-no-good smile
- *Yim cheua-cheuan*   The I-am-the-winner smile, the smile given to a losing competitor
- *Yim soo*   The smile-in-the-face-of-an-impossible-struggle smile
- *Yim mai awk*   The I'm-trying-to-smile-but-can't smile

You can probably understand now why Thais smile a lot more than foreigners. Enjoy the smiles while you are in Thailand as you will probably miss them when you are back home. But remember not to read too much into any smile, particularly those that occur during situations you consider inappropriate.

Entertaining Business Colleagues

The following is a series of questions that attempts to confirm your ideas about particular areas you are still not sure about, and to recap some of the more important considerations for surviving the Thai social environment.

Is it Acceptable to Smoke?

Thai society does not have the anti-smoking laws and lobby groups that are present in the West. However, in some areas such as enclosed public buildings, it is expected that you do not smoke. Thais are usually too *kreng jai* to say no to your request to smoke, even if they do not want you to, so take this into consideration.

Very few Thai women smoke and they never smoke while walking on the street.

What about Alcohol?

There are no social taboos in Buddhist Thailand against drinking. Men usually drink whiskey, of which there are many brands. Imported brands are more popular in business social circles. Imported whisky is often regarded as a status symbol and is a popular gift item. When giving a bottle of whiskey to Thai colleagues, be sure you give a good imported brand like Johnny Walker Black Label at least.

A popular drink at the restaurant table is whiskey mixed with soda water and ice. A word of caution: in some restaurants, waiters make sure that your glass is always kept full, so it is extremely difficult to keep track of how much you are drinking.

Local and imported brands of beer are also popular. In some restaurants, they will bring warm bottles of beer to your table, which you will pour into a glass with ice. Wine is becoming more popular in Bangkok as Thais become more and more accustomed to foreign cuisine and the mandatory glass of wine.

Thai women tend to drink less than their male counterparts but this is changing. On Thai television, an advertisement for a wine cooler features the tagline, "women's only drink".

When Dining with a Colleague, Who Pays the Bill?

In Thailand, the senior person or the person who suggested the dinner will usually pay for the meal. If you are eating with an equal, there may be some confusion as to who should pay but generally, to be polite, you should offer. If both of you insist on paying the bill, suggest you pay this time and your colleague the next time. This usually brings a good response as it suggests your interest in enjoying a meal again with your colleague. The western habit of splitting the bill or "American share" as the Thais call it, is generally inappropriate. In suggesting this, one may appear to be too tight with money.

Should I Leave a Tip in Restaurants?

In some Western countries, you are expected to leave a certain percentage of the bill as a tip. In Thailand, this is not so and it is totally up to your discretion whether to tip or not. If you are going to tip, you should check the bill first because some better restaurants and hotels automatically add a 10% service charge on the bill.

On Business Trips to Thailand, What Type of Hotel Should I Stay In?

The hotel you stay at will somewhat reflect on your status. However, there is no need to go to one of the top-end hotels—a three or four star hotel will do for a business trip. If you think you can get away with staying at a local guest house, you may be in for a surprise—Thais have a habit of asking personal questions.

What if a Thai Male Colleague Invites Me to a Massage Parlour?

If you are a lone male business traveller in Thailand, this topic is likely to come up. Unfortunately in Thailand, the countryside poverty and the status of rural women feed the many brothels in Bangkok. When a Thai invites you to go for a massage, expect to get a lot more than a back rubdown to soothe aching muscles. Remember that many cocktail lounges and karaoke bars are just a front for brothels.

If your prefer not to go, after considering the AIDS problem in Thailand, do not start preaching about your moral values and stomp out the door. Use the discreet, non-confrontational Thai way of getting out of the situation. For example, suggest to your colleague that you have read in the travel guides about Bangkok's famous seafood and you would like to try some on one of your last free evenings before returning home. This not only gets you out of a corner but leaves your colleague with a compliment of his country's fine cuisine.

What Is Considered Appropriate Attire in a Business Setting?

In the West, people believe that "You can't judge a book by its cover". But for the Thais, a neat appearance and dressing for the occasion is a way of expressing goodwill to another. When the Thai dresses neatly, he is saying, "I see you as an important person so I want to dress neatly for you". Clothing should be clean, neat and modest. Despite the heat, men generally wear long pants. Businesswomen stay away from short skirts and tightfitting blouses. In the office, it is acceptable to wear short-sleeved shirts and blouses, and men may sometimes get away with not wearing a tie. For formal occasions gushing with status, always "overdress" in your best attire, including polished shoes, a good watch, and perhaps a silk scarf or necktie.

What Behaviour do Thais Expect from Visiting Business People?

Thais are very polite people and you should try to be polite as well. Even when Thais dislike a person, they will nevertheless be polite to that person. Make a special note of keeping your hands to yourself and avoid making too many gestures.

The Thais have a saying "When in wink town, wink too". This is the equivalent of the English idiom "When in Rome, do as the Romans do". Thais know that foreigners will make many mistakes and are willing to overlook them, but the more you try to adapt to conventional behaviour without compromising yourself, the better you will be received.

What about Dining Table Etiquette?

Thais use mainly spoons and forks when having food. Knives are seldom used except in Western-style restaurants. Chopsticks, together with a spoon, are usually used when eating bowls of noodles—the chopsticks are used with one hand to pick up the noodles and to push food onto the spoon that is held with the other hand.

After a meal, it is socially acceptable to use a toothpick to clean your teeth in Thailand. Thais will happily sit around a table chatting away while picking at their teeth. They will usually use their hand or a serviette to cover their mouth while they do it. However, Thais have a problem with people blowing their noses, especially around food. Spitting is not acceptable, although some of the older generation Thai-Chinese have yet to lose this habit.

At a Meeting with a Group of People I do not Know, Why does My Thai Colleague Seldom Introduce Me to Any One of Them?

In Thailand, it is protocol only to be introduced to those who are worthwhile for you to know. This is not done to minimise your chances of meeting others, but if a Thai thinks an introduction to everyone does not serve any purpose, he will not do so. If there is

If you pass a group of people eating, do not be surprised if they invite you to eat with them. To refuse politely, you only need to say that you have already eaten.

someone you feel it would be useful to know, it is quite acceptable to go up to them and say hello.

What about Toilets in Thailand?

In better hotels and restaurants, bathrooms are very similar to what one would find in the West.

However, many of the more basic houses and roadside restaurants in Bangkok, and most houses in the country, have squat toilets. These do not work on an automatic flush system. Water has to be scooped into the bowl from the water jar next to the toilet. Sometimes there will be no toilet paper. In this instance, you will use water from a hose or water jar next to the toilet to wash yourself. Thais use the left hand to wash themselves, which is in accordance with the Thai body hierarchy where the left hand is lower than the right. For everything else, Thais use the right hand. There are not many left-handers in Thailand and foreign left-handers will find it difficult to find golf clubs and baseball mitts for left-handers in the country.

Do not be surprised to see toilet paper in places where foreigners would usually use tissues. These include dining tables in lower market restaurants and hotels, where you will find it sitting in a cylindrical dispenser with a hole in the lid to pull the paper from. Feel free to take as much paper as you like from the dispenser before visiting the toilet.

In most public toilets, there are toilet paper dispensing machines. Otherwise, toilet paper can be purchased—along with soap and other toiletries—from the maid at the entrance collecting the two-baht service charge. As plumbing in Thailand has not been built to cope with a large amount of insoluble matter, a bucket is left next to the toilet for used toilet paper.

How do Showers Work in Thailand?

The word for bathroom in Thai is *hong naam*, which literally means "water room". Except in better hotels that have Western-style bathrooms, the floors of Thai bathrooms are always wet as there is no shower recess or shower curtain to prevent the rest of the bathroom from getting wet. This is probably another reason why Thais do not keep toilet paper in bathrooms.

If you happen to go on an upcountry trip, you may be faced with the traditional way of showering, which is done by scooping water over your body from a large earthen water jar or other such containers. Make sure that you do not use water from the smaller water jar to bathe, as this is used exclusively for rinsing the toilet bowl and washing your buttocks.

Work versus Public Behaviour

You might think that Thais would typically exhibit admirable codes of behaviour. The emphasis on relationships, on not coming into conflict with others and having such an accepting attitude to life would lead you to believe that the Thai social life is very cordial. And of course, one of the first things that a foreigner notices on arriving in Thailand is how often everyone smiles. The newly-arrived thinks that the phrase "The Land of Smiles" is entirely appropriate in describing this friendly country.

However, the foreigner will start noticing that Thais have almost a double personality. You will notice when you go shopping that people will push to get in front of others rather than queue up to be served. Trying to board a bus to get to work during the rush hour is like being in a rugby scrum. People seem to have no respect for one another on the roads and all Thai social graces are thrown out the window as soon as they get behind a steering wheel. People litter everywhere. Try and get out of a department store lift—people will be pushing to get in before anyone has had a chance to get out. You start to think, "Is this really the same country?"

Do not be fooled. It does get rough out there but Thais do have reasons for behaving this way. Firstly, with Bangkok being as big and crowded as it is, such behaviour is a survival mechanism. Remember that the majority of your staff have to spend hours each day standing—or sitting if they are lucky—in hot and crowded open-air public buses to get to and from work.

Secondly, back on the farm, one's family is what is most important to the rural Thai. Outside the family, farmers rely heavily on one another for cooperative work groups at planting and harvest time. Then there are particular people in the social hierarchy such as the village school principal and members of the provincial committee with whom it is important to have a good relationship. People see no need to invest time in maintaining relationships with people they do not rely on. Likewise in the city. It is just not necessary to be courteous to people you do not depend on. As long as their relationships with others in the office and family are functioning smoothly, everything is fine.

Another viewpoint is that Thais do not grasp the concept of public interest because it is not inherent in Thai culture. There is no word in Thai to match the English word "public" with its full meaning. The word *satharana* comes closest to it but it does not reflect a shared or common interest. Many Thai people regard *satharana* property as belonging to no one rather than everyone, so no one is interested in protecting it.

Be thankful that Thais regard work as an important part of life where it is necessary to be polite!

A Parting Word

Though the rules of behaviour are complicated, the essence of Thai nature is tolerance. Thais do not expect foreigners to become experts in the knowledge and practice of Thai culture. This is provided they do not do anything too outrageous (and even if they do), foreigners will be accepted. In addition, foreigners with a range of skills are likely to be considered *geng* (clever) and admired by Thais, who tend to have mental barriers towards subjects outside their main areas of knowledge.

Thais also admire foreign technology, which is generally considered superior to their own and are complimentary of the technologists who create such technology. Thai culture has survived foreign influence for many centuries, during which time the country has eagerly absorbed foreign technical and commercial techniques. The Thai attitude towards foreign influence shows no sign of change. On the one hand, the country welcomes progress, and on the other, it maintains traditions that have conferred on Thailand its unique identity. Foreign businesses established in Thailand have been successful, and there is no reason to expect this pattern not to continue.

Basic Facts and Travel Tips

Business Hours

Government office hours are from 8.30 a.m. to 12.00 p.m. and 1.00 p.m. to 4:30 p.m. from Monday to Friday. Banks are open from 9:30 a.m. to 3:30 p.m. from Monday to Friday.

Climate

The climate of Thailand is tropical except in the northern highlands, where it is temperate. As a relatively large country stretching over 85 degrees of latitude, there are three distinct climates in Thailand.

Southern Thailand, in particular, is subject to the monsoon season. Here, two seasons are distinguished—the rainy season from May to November and the dry season from December to April. Some people consider Central Thailand to have three seasons—the wet season (July to October), the cool season (November to February) and the hot season (March to June). Basically, Bangkok is hot and humid throughout the year, and December and January are the most pleasant months. Thailand is most prone to floods between September and October. The climate in the north of the country, which has both higher altitude and is further from the equator, is more temperate than the rest of the country.

Currency

The currency of Thailand is the baht, with the satang as the minor unit with a value that is one-hundredth of a baht. Since the baht is a low value currency, the satang is almost worthless. Most prices are quoted to the nearest baht, with the 25 satang coin the lowest value coin in circulation. Baht coins in circulation include one, five and ten baht coins. Notes for 10 baht, still circulating, are being replaced by coins. Higher value notes include the 20, 50, 100, 500 and 1,000 baht notes.

Date and Time
Thai time is seven hours ahead of GMT. There is no daylight saving in summer and the entire country is in the same time zone. There are two systems of counting years in the country—the number of years after the birth of Christ and the number of years after the birth of Buddha. The difference between these two systems is 243 years, with Buddha's birth being earlier. You might find one, the other or both years identified on different documents.

Electricity, Television and Video Standards
Voltage at point of use is 240 v 50 Hz single phase or 415 v 50 Hz three phase. For domestic use, round two-pin plugs with no earth are used. These have limited positive mechanical engagement and are notorious for dropping out of sockets and plunging your computer into darkness. Power supply is not of a particularly high quality, with a high incidence of voltage variation and power failures. Wire fuses are common in domestic installations, with breakers being more common in commercial installation. Power boards in common use domestically and commercially also incorporate separate overload protection.

Like many other countries, computers are extremely commonplace. It is unlikely that you will not be able to gain access to a computer to run the disks you choose to bring with you.

Geography
On its western side, Thailand joins the Malaysian Peninsula. On the east, the country borders Cambodia and Laos on the mainland of Asia. The country of Myanmar (Burma) lies beyond the northern and western border of Thailand. The country has two seacoasts, one on the Gulf of Thailand, including its eastern and western

coastlines and one on the western shores of the Andaman Sea of the Indian Ocean. Much of the country is situated in the fertile drainage basin of its main river system, the Chao Phraya, which empties into the Gulf of Thailand near the capital city of Bangkok.

Hotels

Many international hotels are present in Thailand, at standard five-star prices. In fact, the Royal Orchid Hotel, which is situated on the left bank of the Chao Phraya River in Bangkok, has been consistently voted the best hotel in Asia. Also available are lower range hotels with modest standards and commensurate prices. The tourism boom, sustained at 16% for many years, has encouraged an equivalent rate of expansion in the number of hotel rooms, which has been accommodated by the booming construction sector. There is ample supply of hotel accommodation across Thailand, at very competitive rates by international standards.

Immigration and Visa Requirements

Nationals from 56 specified countries can now stay in Thailand for up to 30 days without an entry visa. For visitors from 76 other countries, visas valid for 15 days may be obtained on arrival at any of the four international airports (Don Muang, Chiang Mai, Ban Hat Yai and Phuket). Categories of visas to Thailand are: transit, visitor transit, tourist, non-immigrant, immigrant and non-quota immigrant. Check with the Thai embassy in your country to determine which list you are on and how long you can stay. Holders of transit, visitor transit and tourist visas are not allowed to work in Thailand.

Normally, you can apply for a three-month working visa in your country's Thai embassy on behalf of employees you wish to send to work in the enterprise in Thailand. A letter from the hiring company in Thailand giving reasons justifying the employment of the foreigner is required to support the visa application.

Matters of Interest To Visitors To Thailand

Health Regulations	Tetanus shots recommended, anti-malaria shots for northern Thailand
Visa Requirements	Transit (1 month), tourist (2 months), non-immigrant (3 months), non-quota immigrant (1 year) and immigrants
Airport Tax	250 baht (but increases expected)
Driving Licence	International licence
Local Currency	Baht (value fluctuates)
Use of Credit Cards	Most are accepted (5% sometimes added to AMEX)
Money Changers	Banks and ATMs, hotels, street vendors

Public Holidays in Thailand:

Watch your calendar—many of the holidays are not fixed and change from year to year.

- 1 Jan   New Year's Day
- February   Makha Bucha or Full Moon Day*
- February   Chinese New Year*
- 6 April   Chakri Day
- April   Songkran Festival or Traditional Thai New Year*
- May   Annual Plowing Ceremony*
- 5 May   Coronation Day
- May   Wiskha Bucha or May Full Moon Day
- July   Asanaha Bucha or Full Moon Day
- 12 August   Her Majesty the Queen's Birthday.
- October   Vegetarian Festival*
- 23 October Chulalongkorn Day
- November   Loi Krathong*
- 5 December The King's Birthday

- 10 Dec Constitution Day
- 31 December New Year's Eve

* Dates of festivals follow the lunar calendar and are not fixed.

Schools

There are special foreign language schools in Bangkok for children of expatriate parents. For the local population, the education system comprises one or two years of pre-school, six years of compulsory primary education, and six years of secondary education, followed by higher education. Secondary education is divided into technical and academic branches.

Education in Thailand suffers from a learn-by-rote reputation though this may not apply to foreign language schools, particularly those affiliated with a foreign institution of learning.

The book *International Schools in Thailand*, written by Jennifer Sharples and Colin De'Ath, is a good place to begin your search for a suitable school for your child.

Shopping

There are no regulations regarding shopping hours in Thailand. Shopping malls usually open late in the morning at about 10 or 11 and stay open until about nine in the evening.

Most products bought in Thailand do not have warranties and 10% VAT will be added in the more reputable shops. Test all electrical merchandise before buying it.

Avoid what appears to be "a steal" when buying gold or gems— it probably is.

Travelling inside Thailand

Extensive bus services exist throughout the country. A limited railway system operates in most of the major population centres. Thai Airways International and Bangkok Airways provide a local network of flights to popular destinations such as Chiang Mai, Phuket and Pattaya.

Travelling to Thailand

The main airport is Bangkok International Airport (Don Muang). Additional airports offering immigration facilities are located at tourist entry points at Phuket, Chiang Mai and Ban Hat Yai.

Thailand is also accessible by train from Malaysia situated at the south of Thailand, where the eastern Asian Express provides a worthwhile travel experience.

Directory of Important Contacts

Banks

Bangkok Bank Ltd.
9 Silom Road, Plabplachai
Bangkok
Tel: 662-231 4333
Fax: 662-231 5451

Bank of Thailand
Bangkhunprom, Phranakorn
Bangkok
Tel: 662-282 3322
Fax: 662-280 0449

Bank of Tokyo Ltd.
62 Silom Road
Bangkok
Tel: 662-236 0119

Banque Nationale De Paris
208 Wireless Road
Bangkok
Tel: 662-651 5678
Fax: 662-651 5688

Chase Manhattan Bank (The)
20 North Sathorn Road
Bangkok
Tel: 662-235 7978

Government Housing Bank
77 Rajadamnern Road, Bangkok
Tel: 662-281 5155/281 5160

Government Savings Bank
470 Phaholyothin Road,
Bangkok
Tel: 662-299 8800
Fax: 662-278 5102

Hong Kong and Shanghai
Banking Corporation (The)
64 Silom Road
Bangkok
Tel: 662-251 3196
Fax: 662-236 7687

International Commercial Bank
of China (The)
36/12 Asoke, Dindaeng
Bangkok
Tel: 662-259 2000
Fax: 662-259 1330

Krung Thai Bank Ltd.
35 Sukhumvit Road
Phakhanong, Bangkok
Tel: 662-255 2222
Fax: 662-389 0826

Thai Farmers Bank
142 Silom Road
Bangkok
Tel: 662-234 7050
Fax: 662-234 7445

World Bank
Udom Vidhya Building
Rama 4 Road
Bangkok
Tel: 662-235 5302

Thai Military Bank Ltd.
3000 Phaholyothin
Bangkok
Tel: 662-299 1111

The English Bangkok phone directory has a full list of banks. Most overseas banks have branches in Bangkok.

The Board of Investment
555 Vipavadee Rangsit Road
Bangkok, Thailand 10900
Tel: (662) 537 8111
Fax: (662) 537 8177

The BOI also has overseas offices in several countries, including Australia, Japan and the United States.

Government Offices
Office of the Prime Minister
Government House
Nakkon Pathom Road
Bangkok 10300
Tel: 281-2500
Fax: 282-0773

Ministry of Agriculture
and Cooperative
Rajadamnoen Road
Bangkok 10200
Tel: 281-5955
Fax: 282-4450

Ministry of Commerce
Sanamchai Road
Bangkok 10200
Tel: 225-8411
Fax: 224-0915

Ministry of Transport
and Communications
Rajadamoen Nok Road
Tel: 281-3422
Fax: 281-1983

Ministry of Education
Rajadamnoen Nok Road
Bangkok 10300
Tel: 282-9893
Fax: 280-0318

Ministry of Finance
Rama VI Road
Bangkok 1400
Tel: 273-9021
Fax: 273-9408

Ministry of Foreign Affairs
Wang Saranrom
Sanamchai Road
Tel: 225-0096
Fax: 226-0285

Ministry of Industry
Rama VI Road
Ratchthewi, 10400
Tel: 246-8106

Ministry of the Interior
Asadang Road
Bangkok 10200
Tel: 222-1141
Fax: 221-0823

Ministry of Justice
Rachadahisek Road
Chattuchak, 10900
Tel: 541-2284
Fax: 224-7278

Ministry of Labour and
Social Welfare
Mitmaitri Road
Dindaeng 10400
Tel: 245-4782
Fax: 245-4782

Ministry of Public Health
Tivanon Road
Nonthaburi 1100
Tel: 591-8536
Fax: 591-8536

Ministry of Science,
Technology and Environment
Rama VI Road
Ratchthewi 10400
Tel: 246-0064
Fax: 246-8106

Ministry of University Affairs
Sriayuthaya Road
Bangkok 10400
Tel: 246-0025
Fax: 245-8636

For further information, please check with the Thai Embassies in your country. They are a great source of information regarding Thailand and the procedures involved when establishing a business in the country.

Recommended Reading

Books

Asian Development Bank, *Asian Development Outlook*, Thailand, 1993.

Baker, Chris and Pasuk Phongpaichit, *Thailand's Boom!*, Silkworm Books, Thailand, 1996.

Bangkok Legal Consultant Ltd., *Doing Business in Thailand*, Bangkok Legal Consultant Ltd., Thailand, 1996.

BIC Publishing Co., Ltd., *Setting up in Thailand. A Guide for Investors*, Thailand, 1990.

Board of Trade of Thailand, *Export and Import Directory*, Government Printing, Thailand (annual publication).

Campbell, Stuart and Chuan Shaweevongs, *The Fundamentals of the Thai Language* (Fifth Edition), Marketing Media Associates Co., Thailand, 1957.

Ch'ng, David C. L., *The Overseas Chinese Entrepreneurs in East Asia*, 1993 Committee for Economic Development of Australia, Thailand, 1993.

Cooper, Donald F., *Thailand Dictatorship or Democracy*, Minerva Press, England, 1995.

Cooper, Robert and Cooper, Nanthapa, *Culture Shock:Thailand*, Times Editions, Singapore, 1996.

Cooper, Robert, *Thais Mean Business*, Times Books International, Singapore, 1991.

Dixson, Chris, *Southeast Asia in the World Economy*, Cambridge University Press, England, 1991.

Hall, Denise, *Business Prospects in Thailand*, Prentice Hall, Singapore, 1996.

Holmes, Henry and Tangtongtavy, Suchada, *Working with the Thais*, White Lotus Co., Ltd, Thailand, 1996.

Hummel, Anita Louise, and Pisces Sethsathira, *Starting and Operating a Business in Thailand*, McGraw Hill, Thailand, 1996.

Kompas Thailand Usid/Kompass Publications, Germany, 1995.

Management Information Services, *Pocket Thailand in Figures*, Alpha Research, 1994.

Management Information Services, *Thailand in Figures, 1995-6*, Alpha Research, Thailand, 1995.

Manilerd, Dr. Chaleo, *Thai Customs and Beliefs*, The Office of the National Culture Commision, Ministry of Education, Thailand, 1988.

Moore, Christopher G., *Heart Talk*, White Lotus Co., Ltd, 1992.

Naisbitt, John, *Megatrends Asia*, Nicholas Brealey Publishing, London, 1996.

Office of the Prime Minister, *Thailand in the 90's*, The National Identity Office, 1995.

Seagrave, Sterling, *Lords of the Rim*, Corgi Books, England, 1995.

Segaller, Denis, *More Thai Ways*, Asia Books, Thailand, 1989.

Segaller, Denis, *Thai Ways*, Asia Books, Thailand, 1989.

Sethaputra, So, *New Model Thai—English Dictionary*, Thai Watana Panich Press Co., Ltd, 1965.

Sharples, Jennie, *Successful Living in Thailand*, Community Services of Bangkok, Thailand, 1989.

Wyatt, David K., *Thailand, A Short History*, Silkworm Books, Thailand, 1982.

Internet Sites

Thailand Real Estates
http://asiabiz.com/thailand/business/realagen. BC
Includes information of Thailand business services and real estate.

Business Travel FAQs
http://www.accessasia.com
An FAQ (frequently asked questions) on Thailand covering topics such as visa requirements, acceptable credit cards, car rental information and geography.

Asian Net—Navigation Map
http://www.asiannet.com/map
AsianNet—the largest source of Asian Information on the internet. AsianNet features information on business, government, education, and culture and the arts, with directories for countries such as Taiwan, Japan, China, Singapore, Hong Kong, Korea, Thailand, Philippines and Malaysia.

http://www.bangkoknet.com/guide/advertin.
Advertising Industry NetGuide to Bangkok.

http://www.corprateinformation.com/thcorp.html

http://www.eden.rutgers.edu/~boon/thaipage.html

http://www.siam.net/indexhb.html
A complete resource centre for information about the kingdom of Thailand, including business, real estate, travel and Thailand's first job fair.

http://www.sino.net/thai/asia
Information on doing business In Thailand.

About the Authors

BEA TOEWS currently combines two long-standing interests—business and education—in an International School in Thailand. She was born in Canada, where she obtained her Bachelors in Arts and Education. She later immigrated to Australia and completed her Masters in Education and Business there.

She has taught in various schools and colleges in Canada, Australia and Thailand. She has also managed a restaurant and several bookshops in Australia as well as written a business English programme for a bank and an executive English programme for a research institute in Thailand. Her other published work is *Succeed in Business: Australia* (Times Editions), which she co-wrote with Peter North, an economist.

ROBERT MCGREGOR was born in Australia, where he obtained a Bachelor of Business degree. He first came to Thailand in 1988 as an AFS High School exchange student. Over the decade, he has accumulated almost five years of experience in Thailand—travelling the country, studying the language and gaining valuable work experience. He has worked in the office of the Australian Embassy in Bangkok and now works as a promotions manager at an international school in Bangkok.

Index